INVINCIBLE

Mental Toughness Techniques for the Street, Battlefield, and Playing Field

A Performance Guide for Athletes and Warriors

SAMMY FRANCO

Also by Sammy Franco

Unleash Hell: A Step-by-Step Guide to Devastating Widow Maker Combinations
Feral Fighting: Advanced Widow Maker Fighting Techniques
The Widow Maker Program: Extreme Self-Defense for Deadly Force Situations
Maximum Damage: Hidden Secrets Behind Brutal Fighting Combinations
Stand and Deliver: A Street Warrior's Guide to Tactical Combat Stances
First Strike: End a Fight in Ten Seconds or Less!
The Bigger They Are, The Harder They Fall
Self-Defense Tips and Tricks
Kubotan Power: Quick & Simple Steps to Mastering the Kubotan Keychain
The Complete Body Opponent Bag Book
Heavy Bag Training: Boxing, Mixed Martial Arts & Self-Defense
Gun Safety: For Home Defense and Concealed Carry
Out of the Cage: A Guide to Beating a Mixed Martial Artist on the Street
Warrior Wisdom: Inspiring Ideas from the World's Greatest Warriors
Judge, Jury and Executioner
Savage Street Fighting: Tactical Savagery as a Last Resort
War Machine: How to Transform Yourself Into a Vicious and Deadly Street Fighter
1001 Street Fighting Secrets
When Seconds Count: Self-Defense for the Real World
Killer Instinct: Unarmed Combat for Street Survival
Street Lethal: Unarmed Urban Combat

Invincible: Mental Toughness Techniques for the Street, Battlefield and Playing Field

Copyright © 2015 by Sammy Franco
ISBN: 978-1-941845-13-4
Printed in the United States of America

Published by Contemporary Fighting Arts, LLC.
Visit us Online at: **www.SammyFranco.com**
Follow us on Twitter: **@RealSammyFranco**

For author interviews or publicity information, please send inquiries in care of the publisher.

Contents

"You have power over your mind - not outside events. Realize this, and you will find strength."

- **Marcus Aurelius**

Warning!

The author, publisher, and distributors of this book disclaim any liability from loss, injury, or damage, personal or otherwise, resulting from the information and procedures in this book. This book is for academic study only.

The information contained in this book is not designed to diagnose, treat, or manage any psychological or physical health conditions.

Before you begin any exercise or activity, both physical and mental, including those suggested in this book, it is important to check with your physician to see if you have any condition that might be aggravated by strenuous training.

Why you should read this book!

Invincible contains battle-tested techniques and strategies for improving mental toughness in all aspects of life. It teaches you how to unlock the true power of your mind and achieve success in sports, high-risk professions, self-defense, fitness, and other peak performance activities.

However, you don't have to be an athlete or warrior to benefit from this unique mental toughness book. In fact, the mental skills featured in this indispensable program can be used by anyone who wants to reach their full potential in life.

Unlike other mental toughness books, Invincible doesn't bog you down with dry theories, mind-numbing case studies, confusing jargon or pointless anecdotal stories. Instead, it's written in simple, easily understood language, so you can quickly learn and apply the mental skills and achieve personal success.

Invincible has grit! It contains fresh and innovative training methods for developing and sharpening the essential building blocks of mental toughness. The techniques and exercises featured in this book are based on my 30+ years of research, training and teaching the martial arts and combat sciences. They have helped thousands of my students excel and achieve their personal goals, and I'm confident they will help you reach new levels of success.

In this comprehensive book, you'll find step-by-step strategies for dealing with the debilitating fear and anxiety often associated with high-performance situations. In essence, it provides you with the mental body armor necessary to cope, perform and prevail from all forms of extreme adversity. By studying and practicing the concepts and principles in this book, you will feel a renewed sense of empowerment, enabling you to live life with greater self-confidence and personal freedom.

Invincible has eight chapters, each one covers a critical aspect of mental toughness. In addition, I have included a glossary of terms and appendix. Since this is both a skill-building workbook and mental training guide, feel free to write in the margins, underline passages, and dog-ear the pages.

Finally, I encourage you to read this book from beginning to end, chapter by chapter. Only after you have read the entire book should you treat it as a reference and skip around, reading those chapters or topics that directly apply to you.

Train hard!

- *Sammy Franco*

Invincible Defined

invincible:

- adjective.

1. incapable of being conquered, defeated or subdued.

2. insuperable; insurmountable

Chapter One
The Power of Mental Toughness

"You must either conquer and rule or serve and lose, suffer or triumph, be the anvil or the hammer."

- Goethe

What is Mental Toughness?

Ask ten people what it means to be mentally tough, and you will likely get ten different answers. This is because mental toughness is a vague and subjective term that is difficult to validate. In fact, no two definitions of mental toughness will ever be exact.

Therefore, for the purposes of this book, I'm going to give you my interpretation of mental toughness based on my personal experiences and observations. Essentially, mental toughness is a performance mechanism utilizing a collection of mental qualities that allows a person to cope, perform and prevail through the stress of extreme adversity. Mental toughness is also a form of self-mastery that plays an essential role in determining optimal performance and success in combat, sports, health, and other important aspects of life. Like any skill or attribute, mental toughness is something that can be learned and developed.

Unfortunately, many people use the term "mental toughness" too loosely. Some self-appointed experts claim that it's simply a collection of positive qualities that help a person cope with a tough situation. For example, this might include something as trivial as preparing for a midterm exam or working in a competitive business environment. Unfortunately, such a cavalier interpretation is misleading and weakens the very essence of this vital performance mechanism.

Finally, not every form of mental toughness is alike. For instance, the mental resilience necessary to survive a prisoner-of-war camp is dramatically different from than the mental strength required to endure and complete the Marathon des Sables. While the two might share similar mental toughness attributes, they are drastically different experiences, requiring dissimilar forms of training.

The Six Elements of Extreme Adversity

Genuine mental toughness is demonstrated when you are confronted with an extreme form of adversity. Examples would include, competing against a superior opponent or performing a mission critical task in a hostile and dangerous environment. Generally, extreme adversity will include most of the following six elements:

- A degree of **danger**
- The element of **risk**
- The presence of **fear**
- The possibility of **loss**
- A challenge to your **self-confidence**
- The experience of **pain** (emotional or physical)

In fact, genuine mental strength requires you to activate every fiber of your being (mentally, emotionally, physically, and spiritually). It's no wonder mental toughness is readily identified with elite military units, like the United States Navy SEALs. These elite warriors are the foundation of Naval Special Warfare combat forces. They are considered the best of the best because they are trained to conduct a wide range of Special Operations missions in all types of extreme climates and hostile environments, including the sea, air, and land.

Pictured here, a Navy Special Warfare Trident insignia worn exclusively by U.S. Navy SEALs.

Physical and Psychological Adversity

Extreme adversity can materialize in one of two forms: physical or psychological. Physical adversity requires you to cope and perform during a physically stressful event or circumstance. For example, physical adversity can be a high-risk self-defense situation requiring you to defend against a physically superior adversary in the street. Or, it could be something less menacing like a competitive wrestling match against a powerful and determined opponent. Both of these examples, however, will still require a substantial amount of mental toughness to cope and perform under these circumstances.

Conversely, psychological adversity requires you to cope and perform during a psychologically stressful event or circumstance. For example, it might require you to withstand the psychological torment of a bully or the relentless taunting of a drill sergeant.

Many traditional occupations might also expose you to various forms of psychological adversity. For example, consider a police officer who must confront and diffuse a verbally abusive crowd or a professional athlete who is regularly insulted by overzealous spectators.

Both of these examples require a certain degree of mental

toughness to cope and perform when faced with the stress of adversity. Finally, physical and psychological adversity are not mutually exclusive. More often than not, they are experienced at the same time.

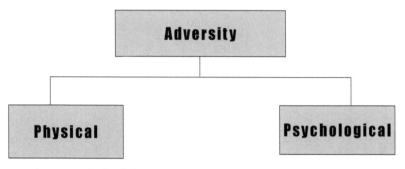

Adversity can be divided into two separate categories: physical and psychological.

Three Objectives of Mental Toughness

Regardless of your occupation, profession or personal goals, mental toughness has three primary objectives. They include the following:

- To *cope* with adversity.
- To *perform* during adversity.
- To *prevail* from adversity.

Coping with Adversity

Mental toughness requires you to accept adverse circumstances. This is counter-intuitive for most people because we are born with a natural instinct to avoid conflict and discomfort. In fact, we often make our situations worse by avoiding them. Therefore, the first step to coping with adversity is to identify and embrace it. Recognize it for what it is - a legitimate obstacle to your goal.

Invincible

Effectively coping with adversity also means you must immediately manage and control the stress that comes with it. This is critical because it determines whether or not you'll be able to perform at the right moment.

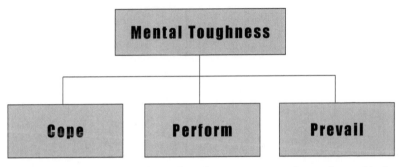

The three primary objectives of mental toughness is to cope, perform and prevail in the face of adversity.

Stress is simply the physiological and psychological arousal caused by a stressor. A stressor is any activity, situation, circumstance, event, experience, or condition that causes a person to experience either physical or mental anxiety. Stressors come in many different forms (mental, physical and emotional), and they can wreck havoc on anyone who is not prepared to handle them.

The first step to manage stress is to observe and acknowledge it. Next, you must immediately prohibit it from affecting your mind and body. You can accomplish this by using a wide range of coping skills, including meditation, mental visualization, positive self-talk, and controlled breathing techniques. Stress inoculation techniques can also be used to minimize stressful events (more will be discussed in a later chapter).

Finally, you must redirect your thoughts and actions to the performance stage of mental toughness. Keep in mind, these three steps are conducted and completed within seconds of identifying the stressor.

Performing in the Face of Adversity

Once you have confronted and accepted adversity and managed the stress associated with it, it's time to take action! Performing under the pressure of adversity will require that your course of action meet three essential requirements: efficiency, effectiveness, and safety.

- **Efficiency** - you course of action is performed in the quickest and most economical fashion.

- **Effectiveness** - your course of action achieves your goal or objective.

- **Safety** -you course of action is performed with the least possible amount of risk or danger.

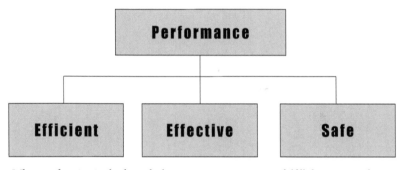

When performing in the face of adversity, your actions must fulfill three essential requirements: efficiency, effectiveness, and safety.

Prevailing in the Face of Adversity

It's not enough to survive through adversity. For example, if you're a police officer engaged in a deadly firefight with the criminal, your ultimate goal is to prevail from the encounter. Similarly, if you are a soldier, your goal might entail defeating a hostile enemy in order to achieve the objectives of your mission. The same concept applies to competitors and athletes. On the field or in the ring, your goal is simple - beat your opponent and win!

Invincible

Chapter Two
The Many Faces of Mental Toughness

"I firmly believe that any man's finest hour - this greatest fulfillment to all he holds dear is that moment when he has worked his heart out in a good cause and lies exhausted on the field of battle, victorious."

-Vince Lombardi

Who Needs Mental Toughness?

Anyone can benefit from mental toughness. However, there are certain people who require it. In fact, mental toughness is an essential tool necessary for many occupations, professions, and activities.

Take a look at America's favorite sport, football. It epitomizes mental toughness. Watch a game and you'll observe some interesting things, like the tremendous power and strength of a 280-pound lineman moving with the speed of a freight train in an all-out effort to crush the quarterback. Pain is exalted; I've heard of a player who continued a game after having torn off his fingertips. You can find other examples of mental toughness in basketball, tennis, hockey, rugby, soccer, martial arts, and various combat sports.

Full-contact sports like football demand a considerable amount of mental toughness.

Mental toughness, however, is not limited to sports. Consider, for example, a rookie police officer fresh out of the academy. There's a very good reason the trainee is accompanied by a field training officer

(FTO) during his initial weeks on the job. Besides teaching and evaluating the rookie, the FTO serves as a role model, mentor, and coach who imparts the mental toughness skills necessary for officer survival.

Here, is a brief list of fields that require mental toughness:

- Military

- Law enforcement

- Self-defense

- Executive and personal protection

- Private security

- Sports and Athletics

- Martial arts

- Fitness and Health

- Self improvement

Two Types of Mental Toughness

Mental toughness skills can be applied to a broad spectrum of circumstances and situations. However, it exists in varying degrees, ranging from mild to extreme. For example, the mental toughness attributes required for a special forces soldier to perform mission critical tasks, will differ from the mental resilience needed to diet, train and compete in the Mr. Olympia. While the two examples might share similar mental toughness attributes, their environment, training, objectives and stressors will differ significantly.

Therefore, there are two broad categories of mental toughness that, in reality, differ in very significant ways: *combative* and *competitive* mental toughness.

Combative Mental Toughness

Combative mental toughness applies to professionals and individuals who must live or work in dangerous and hostile environments, where violence is a very real possibility. Moreover, their occupation requires them to perform high-risk duties while making critical decisions during life-and-death situations. Many of these individuals will face life-threatening encounters on a daily basis. Some include:

- Military personnel
- Law enforcement officer
- Self-defense practitioner
- Security professional
- Doormen or Bouncer
- Bounty hunter

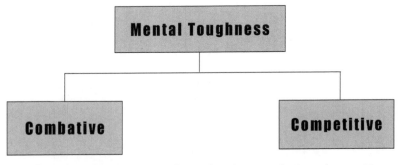

There are two general categories of mental toughness: combative and competitive.

Combative mental toughness is not limited to high-risk occupations. In fact, it's useful to anyone who must confront violence and aggression while risking the possibility of sustaining a severe injury or possible death. Take, for example, a law-abiding citizen who must use deadly force to protect himself and his family from a horrific home invasion. Or perhaps a martial artist who trains and prepares himself for life threatening self-defense encounters.

Finally, combative mental toughness serves as a cognitive survival mechanism for civilians who are forced to live in dangerous and hostile environments. Examples include war zones, prisons, detention centers, mental institutions, and extremely dangerous neighborhoods and districts.

Mental Toughness for Military Service

No one can argue the critical importance of combative mental toughness for military service. From maintaining peace in hot spots around the world to eliminating the enemy, today's modern warrior is required to possess a considerable amount of mental fortitude to withstand the harsh demands of military service. In fact, mental toughness is an essential requirement for all five branches of the United States Armed Forces including:

Invincible

- Army

- Navy

- Marine Corps

- Air Force

- Coast Guard

The physical, emotional, and psychological demands of military service require that all servicemen and servicewomen possess the mental strength necessary to perform their duties. Unlike other professions, a soldier is often required to making critical life-and-death decisions while living in some of the most dangerous environments known to man. Danger lurks everywhere! From the elusive and undetectable sniper to the improvised explosive device (IED), today's serviceman must be vigilant and ready to respond to all forms of danger.

Pictured here, U.S. soldiers engage Taliban forces during a halt to repair a disabled vehicle near the village of Allah Say, Afghanistan.

Chapter Two: The Many Faces of Mental Toughness

In times of war, a professional soldier is expected to engage the enemy. War is, by far, the most horrific thing anyone can experience. For most people, the severity, intensity and unrelenting brutality of war is difficult to imagine and practically impossible to comprehend. The extreme violence, physical destruction, human misery, and death of innocents make it a virtual hell on earth. In order for a soldier to survive the gruesome realities of the modern-day battlefield, he or she must be mentally tough.

U.S. Army Soldiers breach a doorway during a patrol to investigate a house based improvised explosive device that prematurely detonated in Khatoon, Iraq.

Killing the Enemy

A soldier is required to perform a myriad of mission critical tasks, including killing the enemy. This is especially important because today's modern warrior is often compelled to fight the enemy in extremely close quarter urban environments, where long range weapons have limited application. In many instances, the soldier will experience an intimate face-to-face deadly encounter with his or her enemy.

The taking of another life can be difficult, even during a war. In fact, it requires a substantial amount of mental toughness and desensitization to squeeze the trigger, thrust a knife, or lob a grenade at another human being. In combat, a soldier is required to follow orders and act swiftly with absolute clarity. The battlefield is the last place a soldier wants to experience apprehension and self-doubt. A split second of uncertainty can cost his life and perhaps the lives

In this photo, U.S. Army Soldiers clear and patrol the town of Aswad in the Diyala Province of Iraq.

of his brothers in arms. Fortunately, mental toughness provides the mental and emotional clarity necessary to get the job done.

The physical and psychological demands of military service require a soldier to be able to maintain clear thinking under extreme stress. Pictured here, a drill instructor from Marine Corps Recruiting Station Fort Lauderdale corrects a future Marine.

Captured by the Enemy

If the enemy captures a soldier during war, his mental strength will also be challenged. For example, he will most likely be subjected to sleep deprivation, mind games, torture, and starvation. As a prisoner of war, a soldier is required to give his name, rank, serial number, and date of birth. He also has a duty and obligation to avoid answering any other questions. Mental toughness skills are critical at this point because the enemy will do everything possible to get him to talk and provide valuable information. However, with proper training, the soldier will maintain his silence and uphold the requirements set forth by the Armed Forces Code of Conduct.

Returning Home from War

Surviving armed conflicts and completing your military service is just half the battle. The fact is, all veterans who served in war will come back home changed in some significant way. Unfortunately, some will have difficulty transitioning to civilian life while others will suffer the deleterious effects of post-traumatic stress. Regardless, mental toughness skills can be a very useful coping tool to help transition to your new life.

Mental Toughness for Law Enforcement

Law enforcement is another demanding profession requiring a substantial amount of mental toughness. In fact, it can be a very stressful and dangerous job, often requiring the officer or agent to make rapid life and death decisions.

However, police work is not just about patrolling dangerous city streets and arresting bad guys. There are many other aspects of law enforcement that also require a mentally conditioned mind. Some include criminal investigation, SWAT operations, surveillance, undercover work, and hostage negotiation.

The Jack of all Trades

In order to carry out his sworn duties to protect and serve the public, a law enforcement officer must master a wide variety of mental skills and attributes. For instance, one moment he might be resolving a dispute between a merchant and a disgruntled customer, during the next he might be administering first aid to a victim of a horrific traffic accident.

Peace officers must also possess interpersonal skills that allow them to work successfully with the public. For example, they must master the art of "tactical calming" which utilizes both verbal and nonverbal communication skills to assist in diffusing hostile and agitated civilians.

The Importance of Hypervigilance

Law enforcement work is one of the few jobs where violence can erupt without a moments notice. For example, something as seemingly harmless as a traffic stop can instantly turn deadly for the officer. The same applies to domestic disturbance calls and other trivial disputes between citizens. Properly trained police officers are well aware of this fact. They know they must always perform the most innocuous duties with a sense of hypervigilance.

A seasoned police officer knows that one wrong move on the job could easily cost him his life. Officers quickly learn that their immediate environment is potentially deadly. They must always be prepared for the "unknown event" that may put them in harms way.

If a police officer wants to serve safely until retirement, he must always view his immediate surroundings as potentially hazardous. He or she must always be gathering and analyzing information and then accurately evaluating it in terms of threat and danger. Consequently, mental toughness functions as a sobering looking glass for the peace officer by providing him with a no-nonsense, threat-based perspective of his immediate surroundings. Such vigilance wards off the dangerous effects of complacency while simultaneously instilling a sense of duty and pride.

In addition, mental toughness engenders a unique form of situational awareness that permits the officer to observe real-time events as potentially hazardous. It's this form of mental conditioning that allows the officer to rapidly gather and analyze information and then accurately evaluate it in terms of threat and danger.

The ability to accurately assess people, places, actions, and objects is critical for some of the following reasons:

- It significantly enhances officer and public safety.

- It helps the officer or agent determine the appropriate level of force for the situation.

- It helps the officer choose the appropriate tactical option.

How would you rate the focus and concentration of the officer at the bottom?

Finally, mental toughness allows the officer to control and channel the adrenaline dump that accompanies life-and-death encounters. As a result, he can better cope and perform through traumatic armed and unarmed encounters.

Mental Toughness Security Work

Mental toughness is also essential for individuals who work in the private security industry. Unlike professional law enforcement officers, security specialists are civilians who are paid to protect people, assets, and private property. Security work can include a wide range of jobs and occupations. Some include:

- Uniformed Security Officer
- Bouncers/Doorman
- Bodyguards
- Executive Protection Specialist

Security work will also require you to work in a wide variety of venues. Some include:

- Bars
- Nightclubs
- Casinos
- Concerts
- Schools
- Malls
- Shopping Centers
- Arenas
- Theme Parks

The private security field is frequently associated with negative connotations. I'm sure at one time of another you've heard a security officer referred to as a "mall cop" or "rent-a-cop." Or perhaps you've seen it in movies. For example, the entertainment industry is notorious for stereotyping security guards as lazy, fat, insecure, stupid, and unqualified. While I'm certain there is security personnel who might fit these criteria, there are many others who are just as competent and professional as a sworn police officer.

More Dangerous Than Police Work?

Ironically, many forms of security work require the very same skills and attributes of law enforcement. By the same token, private security work can sometimes be more dangerous than traditional law enforcement.

For example, consider the hazardous job of a bouncer or doorman. As a general rule, bouncers are unarmed, outnumbered and have significant use-of-force restrictions imposed by their employers. They frequently work in noisy, dark and crowded environments, filled with intoxicated and belligerent patrons looking to have a "good time." On any given night, a bouncer or "cooler" is likely to encounter pugnacious and lawless individuals looking to prove themselves. In addition, many bars and watering holes are safe havens for depraved criminals and gang members to congregate. So it's no wonder why doormen and bouncers are usually large, powerful, and intimidating looking.

I can tell you, from first-hand experience, that bouncing can be an extremely dangerous job that can cost your life. Here's a true story that took place several weeks after I stopped working as a head bouncer at a Gentleman's Club in Washington, DC. A few weeks after I quit, a new head doorman was hired and was later viciously murdered by one of the patrons. However, what's even more disturbing was the manner in which the bouncer was attacked.

Apparently, after being thrown out of the club for taking photos of a nude dancer, an enraged patron later returned with a can of gasoline and attempted to set the club on fire. When the twenty-six-year-old bouncer tried to stop him, the enraged patron doused him with gasoline and set him on fire. As a result, the bouncer suffered critical burns to 90% of his body, requiring him to undergo dozens of painful surgical procedures. Subsequently, the bouncer died from his injuries, and the patron was sentenced to thirty-five years in prison for arson and murder.

You Have to Stay Sharp!

Security work requires a sharp mind that can make rapid decisions during emergency situations. It's one field that demands both situational awareness and attention control. You cannot afford to be distracted. For example, joking around with people, flirting with girls or playing with your smartphone are classic distractions that quickly put you in harm's way.

Violence can erupt without a moments notice, and you must

always view the people and environment as potentially hazardous. Like police work, you must approach your job with a significant amount of hypervigilance. Likewise, you must anticipate and detect the dangers and threats that come with the job. Fortunately, mental toughness functions as a survival tool that provides a no-nonsense, threat-based perspective of your immediate surroundings. A survival mindset engenders vigilance and helps ward off the dangerous effects of complacency.

Interaction and Confrontation

The vast majority of security work will require you to interact with people. You must possess the interpersonal skills to interact with all types of people across diverse cultures and ethnicities. For instance, you might have to engage and communicate with individuals who are mentally ill, emotionally distraught, hostile, and intoxicated. At times, you might be required to handle difficult and confrontational situations.

It's critical that you always maintain authority over the people who enter your venue or area of responsibility. You must project absolute confidence to the public because anything less can be disastrous. Remember, always do what you say and say what you mean.

Sometimes you will have to confront and challenge people who violate or refuse to comply with the rules of your establishment. In many cases, you will be dealing with hostile individuals who will directly challenge your authority. Some people will resist your power and retaliate with verbal attacks and physical violence.

Mental toughness gives you the mental resilience necessary to deflect verbal abuse while maintaining control over your emotions. Keeping your cool and maintaining a professional demeanor under these conditions is especially important if you are authorized to carry weapons or self-defense devices on the job.

Mental toughness also provides the frame of mind to verbally de-escalate a potentially violent confrontation from erupting. I often refer to de-escalation skills as verbal self-defense. Its goal is to eliminate the possibility of an agitated individual resorting to physical violence. Remember, not every showdown justifies responding with physical force. In fact, there are many instances where you might be required to talk someone out of a fight.

Security works often requires you to confront belligerent individuals who will directly challenge your authority.

Mental toughness provides the clarity and composure necessary to assess a crisis situation and choose a reasonable force response. This skill is especially important if you want to avoid spending time in court or perhaps jail. In America, anybody can sue anybody for anything. Even a criminal attacker can find a legal basis for a lawsuit. You must remember that security work also involves the risk of civil liability and criminal jeopardy. Remember, if you act too quickly or use what others might consider excessive force, you may end up being a defendant in a legal process. If you're not careful with your actions, you can be financially ruined or thrown into jail.

Mental Toughness for Self-Defense

Mental toughness skills are a foundational requirement for self-defense training. In fact, it's is essential for anyone who intends on protecting himself from criminal violence and aggression. Some examples might include:

- Home invasion

- Mugging or Street Assault

- Sexual assault

- Carjacking situation

- Street fight

- Active shooter situation

Performance Requirements for Self-Defense

In order to effectively perform in a self-defense situation, you must master three components or domains of combative preparedness. They include the following:

- **Psychomotor** - being physically prepared for the rigors of combat and possess all of the physical skills, techniques, and attributes necessary to fight effectively, efficiently, and safely.

- **Cognitive** - being mentally and psychologically prepared for the horrors of combat and equipped with the necessary concepts, principles, and knowledge critical for high-risk combat.

- **Affective** - being emotionally and spiritually prepared for the demands and strains of combat, you have philosophically resolved issues related to combat, and your attitudes, ethics, and values are congruent with the task of fighting.

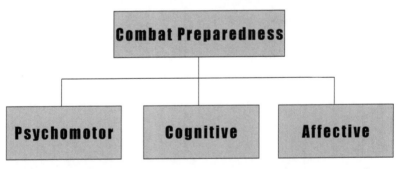

In order to perform in a combat situation, you must master three components of combative preparedness.

Physical Techniques are Not Enough!

While self-defense skills and techniques are a vital part of self-defense training, they are not enough. Physical techniques alone won't prepare you for the stress, anxiety and horrors of real violence. In order to be fully prepared, you must possess a broad range psychological and intellectual skills. In other words, you must equip yourself with the cognitive and affective attributes necessary to perform and prevail against an attacker that is hell-bent on your destruction. In addition, you must also possess the necessary mental coping skills to overcome the fear, anxiety, and inhibitions often associated with physical combat.

Tapping into Your Killer Instinct

Finally, effective self-defense also requires a combat mentality to channel a destructiveness exceeding that of your criminal attacker. Fortunately, mental toughness gives you immediate and direct access to your killer instinct. The killer instinct is a cold, primal mentality that surges to your conscious mind and turns you into a vicious combatant. The killer instinct is a reservoir of energy and strength. It can channel your destructiveness by producing a mental source of cold, destructive power. If necessary, it fuels the determination to fight to the death.

Competitive Mental Toughness

Mental toughness is not just for warriors. In fact, it can help anyone achieve both personal and professional success in our increasingly competitive world. I refer to this as competitive mental toughness. In essence, it permits you to push through the stress and pressure of adversity with the ultimate objective of achieving a personal goal.

Competitive mental toughness is a vital source of power for individuals who want to achieve personal peak performance in any activity or endeavor. This mindset plays a crucial role in determining optimal performance and success in such things as sports, exercise, health, and other important aspects of life. Unlike combat mental toughness, this form of mental strength doesn't entail danger or violence, nor does it require making critical life-and-death decisions.

In this respect, competitive mental toughness is ideal for anyone who wants to be capable of optimum performance while faced with challenging circumstances. Moreover, it can be readily used by anyone, regardless of skill level. For example, it might include high-profile professional athletes, entertainers, weekend warriors, gym rats, distance runners, triathletes, boxers, mixed martial artists, bodybuilders, etc.

Competitive mental toughness also provides additional benefits, including improved self-discipline and self-esteem, enhanced creativity, improved motivation, and a greater sense of autonomy. Finally, possessing this skill and ability to withstand great hardships will benefit anyone who doesn't want to be a slave to fear, apprehension, and self-doubt.

Mental Toughness for Sports

Mental toughness is essential to succeeding in all types of competitive sports. Regardless, if you are playing a team or individual sport, mental toughness provides the psychological edge to outperform your opponent.

Athletes who lack mental toughness will often "choke" and

fall apart from the pressure of a competitive event. Some will get intimidated and psyched out by their opponent, while others abandon their focus and concentration, allowing their imaginations to run wild.

However, an athlete who possesses mental toughness doesn't suffer from these anxieties and problems. Instead, he employs the necessary coping skills to handle the stress and anxiety associated with sports competition. In fact, he views competition from a healthy and productive perspective that makes him remain relaxed under pressure. This state of mental relaxation permits him to enjoy the moment and perform at his peak.

Mental toughness provides a tremendous competitive edge for athletes.

When developed properly, competitive mental toughness provides the athlete with laser-like focus, confidence, and mental clarity to consistently achieve his or her personal goals. Finally, achieving greater levels of sports performance is not an easy task, however mental toughness provides the necessary drive and motivation to compete against yourself and consistently break personal records.

Mental Toughness for Fitness and Health

In sports, as well as many other physical performance activities, complacency often leads to mediocrity. To excel in all types of physical activities, you are required to practice and workout on a regular basis. Unfortunately, there will be mental and physical barriers that will sabotage your training.

For example, you might be going through a mental slump and simply don't feel like working out. Or perhaps, you might be working through a mild and annoying injury that makes you second guess your skills and abilities. You might be dealing with the discomfort of muscle soreness from a previous training session or experiencing family or relationship problems. All of these examples, as trivial as they might seem, can significantly diminish your progress.

Mental toughness, however, gives you the mental resilience to push through these barriers and stay on track with your training regimen. It engenders a vital discipline that allows you to push through discomfort and distractions so that you can complete your workout session.

Getting Motivated

Just about everyone will agree that sticking to a fitness, diet or health program is hard work. In fact, most people fail to achieve their personal goals because they lack the determination and motivation to stay on course.

Failure to achieve personal goals is a result of poor motivation and willpower. However, mental toughness skills will strengthen your mind, making you more motivated and determined to achieve your personal goals. Laziness and negativity are eliminated and replaced with positive energy and a desire and willingness to follow through with your intentions.

Chapter Three
The Nature of the Beast

"If we did the things we are capable of, we would astound ourselves."

-Thomas Edison

Mental Toughness Attributes

Now that you have a general understanding of mental toughness, it's time to delve deeper into this invaluable source of mind power. Mental toughness consists of several interrelated elements know as attributes. Essentially, this collection of attributes can either be *reactive* or *proactive*.

A reactive attribute is a quality that allows you to cope and perform during the immediate stress and pressure of adversity. While a proactive attribute is used to maintain optimum performance under less stressful conditions. Both types of attributes serve as the essential building blocks of mental toughness.

The Mental Toughness Package

During my 30+ years of teaching the combat sciences to law enforcement, military personnel, athletes and people of all backgrounds, I have discovered that a complete mental toughness package consists of the following core attributes.

- **Instrumental Aggression**
- **Assertiveness**
- **Resilience**
- **Self-Confidence**
- **Self-Discipline**
- **Awareness**
- **Attention Control**
- **Philosophical Resolution**
- **Responsibility**
- **Courage**

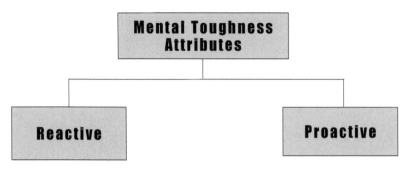

There are two different types of attributes that comprise mental toughness: reactive and proactive

Nature or Nurture

Are mental toughness attributes learned or instinctual? This question has perplexed psychologists and coaches for decades, creating a debate over the nature theory and the nurture theory.

Advocates of the nature theory believe that mental toughness is innately linked to biological, genetic and physiological factors. Built into the machine if you will. On the other hand, advocates of the nurture theory believe that mental toughness is learned from your environment and various other external factors.

The debate between these two schools of thought has gone on for some time and will most likely continue. I strongly believe that mental toughness is a combination of both nature and nurture. The raw instinct for mental toughness was manifested from the beginning of man's existence. It was a vital factor in his survival against nature's brutality, including the threat of other aggressors like himself. His adaption to adversity, accompanied with his unique problem solving abilities seem to be a combination of both genetic factors and environmental influences. Where one influence leaves off and the other picks up is impossible to say.

However, the important point is that mental toughness can be learned and developed. The first step, however, is to recognize and understand its core attributes. Only then can mental toughness be fully developed, and ultimately honed to maximize your performance during critical situations.

Now, let's take a closer look at the individual components of mental toughness. We will start with Instrumental aggression.

Instrumental Aggression

"Aggressive fighting for the right is the noblest sport the world affords."

-Theodore Roosevelt

For many people, the concept of aggression immediately conjures up images of senseless and overt acts of violence directed against another individual. There are others who believe that human aggression is the root of all evil and the primary cause of social conflict and global warfare.

However, human aggression is a necessary behavior trait that has ensured the survival of our species, and it's also a vital component of mental toughness. Essentially, there are two distinct categories of aggression: instrumental and reactive.

- **Instrumental aggression** - purposeful and controlled aggressive action designed to help achieve a particular objective or goal. A police officer arresting a criminal suspect or a bouncer physically ejecting a belligerent patron from a bar, are good examples.

- **Reactive aggression** - impulsive and emotionally charged aggressive action that is provoked by an external source.

For example, a woman who slaps a man for insulting her, is clearly demonstrating reactive aggression. A road rage incident is also another good example of reactive aggression.

Mental toughness regularly requires the application of instrumental aggression. As a matter of fact, I define instrumental aggression as purposeful and controlled violence directed to a specific person while maintaining both strategic and tactical objectives.

Instrumental aggression is particularly important for occupations and activities that require you to administer physical force, such as military service, police work, private security, and self-defense. Full-contact sports like boxing, mixed martial arts, kickboxing, wrestling, football, rugby, lacrosse, roller derby, and ice hockey will also benefit from controlled aggression.

Assertiveness

"Take the place and attitude to which you see your
unquestionable right, and all men acquiesce."

– Emerson

Just about every sporting event or high-risk occupation involves some form of interaction and communication between people. For example, in sports there will be an exchange of words or behaviors between teammates, coaches, family members, and spectators. In high-risk occupations like police work, you might be required to interact with a host of different people including supervisors, co-workers, civilians, and criminals.

In order to perform at your best, you must possess a healthy degree of assertiveness. Assertiveness is a form of behavior characterized as a confident and positive expression of your thoughts, feeling, and needs. On the other hand, it doesn't mean being pushy, intrusive, confrontational, or autocratic.

Highly competitive sporting events are not won by meek individuals. Athletes must possess healthy communication skills. They must be able to express their goals, needs and rights to other teammates and coaches. Failing to assert yourself with both teammates and coaches can be problematic and self-destructive. Actively avoiding unpleasant confrontations or suppressing or denying your feelings can be damaging on many levels, resulting in loss of confidence and self-respect. In addition, you might experience feelings of powerlessness, anger, frustration, anxiousness, and resentment. More importantly, passive communication tells others that you are weak and not to be taken seriously.

Assertiveness skills are also critical for high-risk occupations like police and security work. As a peace officer, your job requires the discretionary use of authority accompanied by an assertive police presence. Your job often requires a definitive and confident response to troublesome people and challenging situations. Assertiveness is a healthy and essential form of communication that allows you to persuade other people to see your goals and needs without alienating or disrespecting them. As a result, you will be able to keep the lines of communication open while performing your duties with a greater level of professionalism.

Assertiveness is also a vital trait in the world of self-defense. The immutable fact is humans, by nature, take full advantage of weak and timid personalities. And it's no surprise that meek people get manipulated and exploited by shrewd and psychologically dominant individuals. Through effective communication skills, you can thwart a person's efforts to intimidate, dominate, and control you.

For example, let's say you're working late at the office, and your co-worker makes sexual advances toward you. In this instance, you would be assertive and confront him. In a firm and confident manner, you would tell him that you're not interested in his advances, and you want him to stop his offensive actions immediately. It's this confident and assertive attitude that makes you less likely to be perceived as an easy mark. Weakness and uncertainty are replaced by confidence and strength. You are seen as self-assured and purposeful and you less likely to be perceived as a victim.

Resilience

"A champion is someone who gets up when he can't."

- Jack Dempsey

Resilience is the ability to recover quickly from various forms of adversity. Essentially, it provides the mental strength to "bounce back" or "get back on your feet" and continue pursuing your goal or objective. For example, an athlete might sustain a physical injury or embarrassing performance mistake. A soldier might experience psychological trauma from war, or a police officer might experience post-traumatic stress from a deadly shootout with the criminal. As diverse as these examples might be, all of them require a substantial amount of mental resilience to recover and get back on track.

Resiliency requires you to be adaptable. You must possess the necessary physical and mental skills to adapt to the rapidly changing circumstances of your environment. In combat, for example, factors and circumstances change like the wind. A prepared combatant knows how and when to adapt to his environment. Adaptability allows one to adjust to new or different conditions or circumstances both physically and psychologically. In the heat of combat, a soldier doesn't have the luxury of questioning change. He or she cannot overly scrutinize a particular situation. In fact, he must simply conform to the immediate demands of his predicament.

Two Types of Resilience

There are two distinct categories of mental resiliency: *immediate* and *reflective.* Let's take a look at each one.

Immediate Resilience

Immediate resilience requires you to adapt immediately to the stress you experience during a crisis or event. For example, consider a professional boxer who encounters an unexpected hook to the head during a match. To stay on his feet and avoid going "down for the count", he must immediately adapt and make the necessary adjustments to regain his equilibrium, balance, and mental composure. During his opponent's flurry of punches that follow suit, the boxer must remain focused and not fold under pressure. It's during this crisis moment, he must demonstrate the immediate resilience to bounce back and endure the pain and emotional anxiety associated with his opponent's vicious assault.

Immediate resilience is particularly important for grueling endurance sports like triathlons, marathons, ultramarathons, and extreme obstacle races. Endurance sports are about mental willpower. They require you to compete against your most formidable opponent - yourself.

In order to perform well, you must possess the mental resilience to cope with the inevitable pain, fatigue, and exhaustion that comes with these types of endurance events. Immediate resilience simply gives you the mental wherewithal to push through these obstacles and win.

Reflective Resilience

Reflective resilience, on the other hand, is the ability to bounce back from setbacks that involve either physical injury or mental trauma. In many ways, it's a form of picking up the pieces and rebounding from adversity. For example, a professional athlete who experiences a serious sports injury might become disheartened and question whether he has the skill and talent to pursue his journey. His despair brings him to a mental crossroad where he must summon the resilience to fight his fears and apprehensions. Reflective resilience provides the athlete with the strength and resolve to work his way back to his previous healthy state. Moreover, with serious thought and honest reflection, the athlete acquires a renewed sense of motivation and commitment.

Finally, reflective resilience is essential for individuals who experience psychological trauma from hazardous duties. Consider a soldier, who experiences the horrors of war might suffer from combat stress reaction (CSR) or a police officer who experiences a traumatic incident might develop post-traumatic stress. Reflective resilience acts as a type of mental armor that protects your psyche and helps you recover from a traumatic event.

Self-Confidence

"They can do all because they think they can."

- Vergil

Successful athletes thrive during high-pressure competition because they are confident they possess the skills and ability necessary to beat their opponents. Their self-confidence serves as an effective coping mechanism to overcome anxiety, self-doubt, intimidation, and fear during a high-performance event.

Self-confidence means having an unshakable trust in both your judgment skills and abilities. However, it should not be confused with arrogance or false bravado. In fact, you must be self-aware. You must have an accurate and realistic perspective of yourself including both your inherent strengths and weaknesses. When all is said and done, dangerous poisons like egotism, conceit and narcissism will undermine your goals by instilling a false reality.

Self-confidence can be infectious and will often have a spillover effect in team sports. For example, an athlete who believes in himself resolutely, often inspires his teammates to push past their limits during difficult circumstances. He might also energize spectators and fans to rally and cheer his team to victory. Conversely, players demonstrating low self-esteem, poor self-image and a lack of confidence can also cripple a team and bring it down to its collective knees.

Staring into the Face of Danger

Self-confidence is both a proactive and reactive tool. For example, in self-defense you need a substantial amount of self-confidence to confront a threatening attacker. Defending yourself against a violent attack requires a tremendous amount of personal faith in your skills and abilities. In this instance, you are demonstrating a reactive form of self-confidence.

Self-confidence can also be proactive. For instance, when walking in public, avoid showing signs of weakness and insecurity. Instead, keep your head up and carry yourself with confidence and purpose. When conversing with people, demonstrate strength and confidence by maintaining direct eye contact. As trivial as they may seem, these proactive forms of self-confidence are vital for your personal safety.

Self-Discipline

"He who conquers others is strong; he who conquers himself is mighty."

–Lao Tse

Self-discipline is considered the single most important trait required to achieve personal excellence. As a matter of fact, it's self-discipline that separates the novice from the expert and the highly accomplished person from the underachiever. Self-discipline is the ability to work methodically and consistently toward a personal goal until it is achieved. In some instances, it might require you to work tirelessly day after day, week after week, and month after month until your objective is actualized.

Self-discipline requires you to control and manage your impulses, emotions and desires so you can effectively pursue and ultimately reach your goals. It means having the self-control to ignore the deleterious temptations of instant gratification, in favor of acquiring a more meaningful and sometimes arduous goal.

Self-discipline does not mean living your life like an ascetic monk or denying yourself worldly pleasures. It doesn't mean limiting or restricting your lifestyle or abstaining from enjoyable things. Rather, self-discipline means focusing your mind exclusively on a goal and directing all of your energy until you achieve your objective.

Self-discipline also means controlling your mind and body with positive and purposeful choices, instead of negative emotions, bad habits, and external influences. Simply put, self-discipline allows you to achieve your goals in a very efficient and effective manner.

The Three Steps of Self-Discipline

Self-discipline is not just a trait, it's also a skill that can be learned. It requires you to take three simple yet effective steps. First, you must make a specific decision. Second, you must take the necessary action for that decision. Third, you must follow-through with the proper course of action (despite the obstacles that come with it) until you achieve your goal or objective.

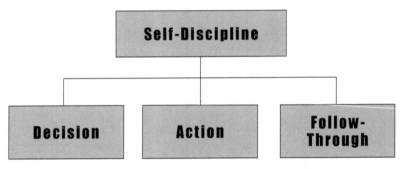

Self-discipline is a relatively simple three stage process.

Other Benefits of Self-Discipline

There are many other benefits of self-discipline, here are a few.

• Self-discipline increases your self-confidence.

• Self-discipline improves your creativity and imagination.

• Self-discipline sharpens and refines analytical thinking.

• Self discipline promotes leadership skills.

• Self-discipline generates respect from other people.

• Self-discipline gives you a greater passion for life.

Self-Discipline Exercises:

1.In your own words, briefly describe what self-discipline means to you.

_____

_____

_____

_____

_____

_____

_____

_____

2. Describe the most self-disciplined person you know and explain his or her success.

_____

_____

_____

_____

_____

_____

_____

_____

3. Describe the least self-disciplined person you know and explain his or her failures.

_____

_____

_____

_____

_____

_____

_____

_____

4. Name three aspects of your life that are in desperate need of self-discipline.

_____

_____

_____

_____

_____

_____

_____

_____

5. Briefly describe three problems you are currently experiencing due to a lack of self-discipline.

_____

_____

_____

_____

_____

_____

_____

_____

6. Describe several benefits you will acquire from developing self-discipline.

_____

_____

_____

_____

_____

_____

_____

_____

_____

_____

Awareness

"The ultimate value of life depends upon awareness and the power of contemplation rather than upon mere survival."

-Aristotle

Your awareness or perception of people, places, actions, and objects is a vital component of mental toughness. In fact, peak performance in every activity or endeavor can only be achieved through the proper awareness skills. Awareness gives you the ability to respond rapidly and successfully to a wide variety of stressful situations and circumstances. In addition, it offers the necessary introspection to identify which aspects of yourself create obstacles that prevent you from achieving your goals.

Your Perception Matters

Awareness is directly linked to your perceptions. Perception is the interpretation of information acquired through one's senses when faced with a stressful or dangerous situation. You gather information through your five senses. Your eyes, ears, nose, and senses of touch and taste will provide a wealth of vital information about your environment. With adequate training, your senses can be sharpened, and your powers of observation enhanced.

The ability to process information varies from person to person. In fact, two people who witness the same event are likely to report it differently. This is referred to as "individual perception." In part, previous experiences can determine the manner in which a person will interpret stimuli. When it comes to achieving peak performance in combat and athletics, you must attempt to remove preconceived notions, assumptions, and biases that may lead to dangerously incorrect conclusions or oversights. These false reactions form barriers to your ability to grasp reality.

Two Types of Awareness

There are two types of awareness that are directly linked to mental toughness. They are: *situational* and *self-awareness*. Let's start by taking a look at situational awareness.

Situational Awareness

Situational awareness is total alertness, presence, and focus on virtually everything in your immediate surroundings. For example, if you are a soldier, police officer or security agent, you must train your senses to detect and assess the people, places, objects, and actions that can pose a danger to you. Do not think of situational awareness simply in terms of the five customary senses of sight, sound, smell, taste, and touch. In addition, the very real powers of instinct and intuition must also be developed and eventually relied upon.

Self-defense clearly illustrates this point. For example, a vagrant congregating by your car, the stranger lingering in your apartment hallway, two men following you in a deserted parking lot, the stray dog ambling toward you in the park, a large limb hanging precariously from a tree... these are all obvious examples of persons, places, and objects that pose a threat to you.

Situational awareness also diminishes the potency of the criminal's favorite weapon - the element of surprise. Your ability to foresee and detect danger will diminish his ability to stalk you, or lie in wait in ambush zones. In addition to enhancing your ability to detect, avoid, and strategically neutralize ambush zones, situational awareness allows you to detect and avoid threats and dangers not necessarily predicated on the element of surprise. Some situations afford potential victims the luxury of seeing trouble coming. Nonetheless, it's remarkable how many people fail to heed obvious signs of danger because of poor awareness skills. They overlook the signals - belligerence, furtiveness, hostility, restlessness - so often manifested by criminal attackers. They neglect the opportunity to cross the street long before the shoulder-to-shoulder encounter with a pack of young toughs moving up the sidewalk. Once it's too late to avoid the confrontation, a whole new range of principles comes quickly into play.

How to Sharpen Your Senses

Your five senses (sight, smell, touch, sound, and taste) can be sharpened through a variety of exercises designed to develop both raw detection and learned identification abilities.

For example, sit on a park bench for a given period of time and catalog the various objects and actions your five senses detect, then list the possible sources of the sensory data. With sufficient practice, you will make significant progress from being unable to detect a particular sound or smell to not only detecting it quickly and accurately, but also identifying its source. Remember that sensory development increases as these exercises are performed in different environmental settings.

Trust Your Instincts

Situational awareness also means trusting your instincts. Learn to rely on your innate ability to know or sense something without the use of rational thought. In many circumstances, immediate cognition will provide you with the necessary time to respond to a challenging or threatening situation. In some situations, going with your "gut" reaction can be just what is called for. Remember, when something doesn't seem right, or the objective data doesn't add up, then chances are something is wrong.

Emotional Recognition Exercise

The objective of this exercise is to sharpen your ability to recognize and identify various emotional states in people. To perform the exercise, spend approximately 20 minutes in a busy public place (i.e., train station, bus stop, sporting event, courtroom, shopping mall, emergency room, airport, etc.), and observe people's emotional states. Pay close attention to their posture, voice, demeanor, hand movements, and facial expressions. Note them in writing.

Combat Situational Awareness Exercises

1. If your occupation requires you to work in potentially dangerous or hostile environments, detect at least ten different ambush zones at your workplace and write them down. Don't pick the obvious ones. It's your life; learn to think like the bad guy.

2. Detect ten different ambush zones in front of your home. If you didn't find ten, you didn't look hard enough.

3. Over the next ten days do not allow yourself to be taken by surprise -by anyone! Every time it happens, record the circumstances: who, what, when, how, where, and why.

4. When you watch television, go to the movies, look at pictures, read books, or play video games, note ambush zones that have not occurred to you in your other assessments. Note them in writing.

5. Visualize five different settings. They can be friendly and familiar like your backyard, or hostile and strange. Write down the things that you have mentally noted in these visualized settings.

6. When observing people in public places, try to identify at least five places on their body where they could be concealing a weapon.

Self-Awareness

Self-awareness has been the subject of philosophers and mystics for centuries. Socrates said, "Know thyself." He believed self-knowledge to be essential to the attainment of true virtue. Self-awareness empowers athletes by giving them invaluable information about their strengths, weaknesses, attitudes, motivations, and beliefs.

Invincible

The key to making positive changes in your behavior and ultimately improving your performance is first to understand yourself in relation to your sport. Self-awareness gives both athletes and warriors the experiential knowledge to control his or her performance during highly stressful events.

Self-awareness involves the harmonious integration of your mind and body to gain full-control of any high-pressure performance situation. It allows you to read, interpret, and understand what your body is telling you. As a result, you remain calm, focused, and in complete control of your emotions when experiencing both performance success and failures.

Moreover, self-awareness helps you mentally recall, imprint, and hopefully replicate the positive experiences of an ideal performance state. Conversely, it also helps you recognize, identify and avoid the negative and unproductive elements that come with a poor performance.

Different Forms of Sports Performance Awareness

- The athlete is focused exclusively on the immediate performance task.

- The athlete makes accurate assessments and adjustments during performance.

- The athlete recognizes his or her limitations while performing.

- The athlete understands the stressors that cause poor performance.

- The athlete is able to control his emotions during performance.

Self-Awareness Questions for Sports Performance

The following questions were designed to start you thinking in the important process of self-awareness. Use them to form an overall personal profile of yourself.

1. What essential qualities do you bring to your sport?
2. What essential qualities do you bring to your team?
3. What separates you from other athletes in your field?
4. What are your feelings (both positive and negative) about your sport?
5. What does performance success mean to you? Give examples.
6. What does performance failure mean to you? Give examples.
7. Exactly how do you feel when you perform at your best?
8. What enables you to perform at your best?
9. What contributes to your performance failures?
10. Exactly how do you feel when you perform poorly?

Self-Awareness for Combat

Self-awareness is also a critical component of combat training and self-defense. For example, what aspects of yourself provoke violence and which, if any, would promote a proper reaction in defense against a threat of violence to you or others? Let's look at certain aspects important to self-protection and ask ourselves a few tough questions.

Physical Attributes

What are your physical strengths and weaknesses? Are you overweight or underweight? Is your body language and the manner in which you carry yourself more likely to provoke or deter a violent attack? Do you have any training in self-defense? Are you fit or out

55

of shape? Do you have the skill to disarm a knife-wielding attacker? Do you smoke or drink excessively? Are you skilled with firearms or edged weapons?

Mental Attributes

What are your mental strengths and weaknesses? Are you an optimist or pessimist? Can you summon up courage and confidence even when you are feeling fearful or insecure? How do you handle stress? Do you panic or frighten easily? Do you have any phobias? What are your fears? Do you think well on your feet?

Communication Skills

What are your strengths and weaknesses in expressing yourself with words? Are you likely to aggravate or diffuse a hostile situation? Are your words congruent with your tone of voice? Can you communicate adequately under stressful situations, or do you become nonplused?

Personality Traits

What type of person are you? Are you passive or aggressive? Are you opinionated and argumentative or open-minded and deliberative? Are you fiery, loud, and boisterous, or quiet, subdued, and calm? Are you quick to anger? Do you harbor grudges? Are there sensitive issues or remarks that may cause you to lose your temper?

Gender and Age

What are the different types of violent crimes that are directed toward you because of your sex? Women are much more likely than men to be raped or abused by their spouses. On the other hand, males are more likely than females to be victims of homicides. Is your age an open invitation for an attack? Children are more likely to be molested or kidnapped than adults, and older adults are weaker and more vulnerable to attack than middle-aged people.

Occupation

Does the nature of your occupation make you or your family vulnerable to different forms of criminal violence? Are you involved with the military or law enforcement? Are you a celebrity? Do you have diplomatic or political connections? Do you control large sums of money or valuable drugs? Does your political affiliation make you or your family a likely target for kidnapping and terrorism?

Income Level

What types of crime are directed toward you because of your income level? Self awareness means knowing and understanding yourself. This includes aspects of yourself which may provoke criminal violence and which will promote a proper and strong reaction to an attack. Are you wealthy, comfortable, or poor? Does your income level make you and your family vulnerable to kidnapping for ransom? Or does your financial situation force you and your family to live in poor neighborhoods that invite violent crime? Are you wealthy and flashy with outward evidence of this wealth?

Self-Awareness Exercises

The following questions will help you recognize the traits that provoke and/or prevent a violent attack.

1. Think of five physical and five mental weaknesses that would inhibit your survival in a self-defense situation.

2. Recall a very stressful situation. How did you react? How did you feel? Were you angry? Did you lose control? Were you calm, notwithstanding the pressure?

3. Ask a close friend or your spouse to evaluate your

communication skills in a variety of situations with other people. Are you open and receptive, rude or polite, emphatic and expressive, or reserved and withdrawn? Do not react defensively to the critique you receive, even if you don't agree.

4. Look into the mirror and conjure up the following mental and emotional states, carefully noting your facial expressions as they arise: anger, happiness, sadness, depression, surprise, and fear.

5. Go back to the preceding exercise and focus on anger. Pay close attention to your facial expressions and other physiological manifestations. What do you see?

6. Think of three forms of violent crime that you may be subject to because of your occupation.

7. Think of three forms of violent crime that you may be subject to because of your gender.

8. To gain a better understanding of yourself, complete the following four exercises. Be frank and truthful.

- Do you believe you could take the life of another human being?

- List four of your greatest fears.

- What steps might you take to eliminate or diminish those fears?

- Name three issues, topics, comments, or situations that would provoke you to lose your temper.

Attention Control

"The field of consciousness is tiny. It accepts only one problem at a time. Get into a fist fight, put your mind on the strategy of the fight, and you will not feel the other fellows punches."

- Saint-Exupéry

Earlier, I discussed situational awareness and its importance for mental toughness. Situational awareness provides the raw data of your immediate surroundings, while attention control is the ability to select what stimuli to pay attention to and what to ignore. Attention control is actually a combination of two mental skills: *selective attention* and *concentration.*

Selective attention is the ability to filter out and ignore the unnecessary sights, sounds, sensations, thoughts, and emotions and focus exclusively on stimuli that is pertinent to your goal or objective. Simply put, it means selecting and discriminating the valuable data that is critically important to your task, from a considerable amount of junk. Concentration, on the other hand, is the ability to sustain attention over a specific period of time.

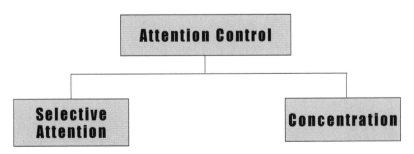

Attention control is a combination of both Selective Attention and Concentration.

Concentration Shifting

Both warriors and athletes are required to shift their attention constantly during critical performance moments. At any given time, they might be required to shift their focus from internal to external or broad to narrow. For example, during a professional fight, a mixed martial artist must first focus his attention internally by develop a winning strategy predicated on his opponent's apparent strengths and weaknesses. Then, he shifts his attention to external factors like the opponent's range, movement, angle of attack, and punch trajectory. Finally, he narrows his focus even further by delivering a precisely timed knockout counter strike.

Two Sources of Distraction

Concentration requires a unified mind that is free from all types of distractions and fully focused on the immediate situation. Distractions are derived from one of two sources. The first is eternal, where in your mind wanders off or panics prior to or during a stressful situation.

The second is external when outside elements force your mind to lose focus. For example, when your opponent attempts to verbally "psych you out" for example. Or when you become physically injured during a dangerous crisis situation. Environmental conditions such as weather, lighting, terrain, and noise can also create external distractions.

For this reason, I teach my students how to avoid being distracted by the opponent during the pre-contact stages of a self-defense altercation. For example, they are taught to disregard such things as psych-out techniques, threatening gestures, eye movements, abusive language, and drastic fluctuations in voice including tone, pitch, tempo, and volume.

Regardless of the source, distractions must be ignored and ultimately eliminated from your consciousness if you are to achieve peak performance in any endeavor.

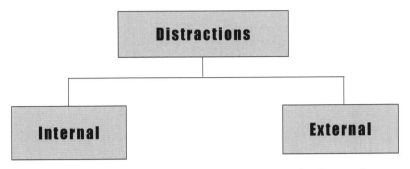

Distractions are derived from one of two source: Internal and External.

Philosophical Resolution

"On the occasion of every act ask thyself: How is this with respect to me? Shall I repent of it? A little time and I am dead, and all is gone. What more do I seek, if what I am now doing is the work of an intelligent living being, and a social being, and one who is under the same law with God?"

- Marcus Aurelius

Mental toughness requires you to address difficult and often controversial questions concerning the use of violence. Philosophical resolution of important martial issues contributes to a warrior's mental confidence and clarity. It is alarming to think of the many years spent by so many warriors achieving the capability to harm others, and even destroy life, with little or no time devoted to the intellectual resolution of questions concerning the ultimate use of violence.

Invincible

Why are you reading this book? What is your greatest fear? What is the source of your spiritual strength, if any? What is the mind, and what does it mean to be conscious? What is the link between mental power and physical activity? Who are you? How do you know right from wrong?

These are only a few vital questions you must resolve honestly and fully before you can advance to the highest levels of combat awareness. If you haven't begun the quest to formulate the important questions and find your answers, then take a break. It's time to figure out just why you want to know the laws and skills of combat.

A Mixed-Up Moral Conscience

Military, law enforcement, security and self-defense practitioners must take the necessary time to resolve moral issues concerning the use of deadly force in combat. Your religious, philosophical or spiritual beliefs must permit you to justifiably take the life of another in battle. As a result, the warrior is free of apprehension and capable of unleashing violence.

Ironically, one of the biggest obstacles in a combat is often a mixed-up moral conscience. For some people, being forced to use deadly force can create apprehension during a life-and-death encounter. This is often because of incorrect perceptions or misinterpretation of many religious or associated beliefs.

Our culture and system of government are both based on the Judeo-Christian ethic. With this in mind, our parents, teachers, and mentors have ingrained morality issues in us. Therefore, such common statements as "pick on someone your own size" or "don't hit a woman" often leave you with the fatal perception that a smaller or female adversary should be treated differently, when, in reality, anyone - regardless of size, age, gender, race, or appearance - has the potential to destroy you. The Bible can also be easily misinterpreted regarding the use of deadly force. This misinterpretation can be identified in two situations.

Hesitation or The Failure to Act

The commandment "Thou shalt not kill" can cause people to hesitate to employ lethal techniques. A more accurate translation of this commandment is "Thou shalt not murder" (Exodus 20:13) (murder being the unjustifiable taking of another human life). Some people feel they have no right to kill another human being. When using deadly force, your objective is not to take life from another human being, but to stop your enemy from causing you grievous bodily harm or possible death. However, the possibility of the enemy dying should be of no consequence to you. The bottom line is when warranted and justified, killing another person is permitted even under God's law.

Guilt

People who justifiably employ deadly force later suffer some degree of guilt over their actions. They often question their right to take another life in defense of their own. They believe that life is sacred and that only God has the right to take it away. However, in the Bible, if someone tries to kill another unjustifiably, he forfeits the sanctity of his life, and he suffers any consequences brought on by his own actions (Exodus 21:12 and 14). God commands us to protect our lives from others that would take it away unjustifiably. At the same time, God removes the sanctity of a person who chooses to attempt to take the life of someone else unjustifiably.

Responsibility

"If you could kick the person in the pants responsible for most of your trouble, you wouldn't sit for a month."

- Theodore Roosevelt

Responsibility is another core component of mental toughness. Essentially, it means being morally accountable for your own behavior. For example, athletes are responsible for their training and game performance as well as their relentless drive to improve themselves. They must consistently evaluate their performance and determine what must be done to eliminate mistakes in order to achieve peak performance. Consequently, they must take full responsibility for each and every decision and action they make during competition. They must take credit and responsibility for both victories and losses alike.

However, warriors and athletes are only responsible for what they control. Unnecessarily blaming yourself for things that are clearly out of your control is fruitless, and in many cases, self-destructive. The truth is you can still lose a game or battle, despite your best efforts.

The Pitfall of Excuses

Likewise, you must also avoid making excuses for performance failures that are clearly your responsibility. The bottom line is, you and only you must take responsibility for your mistakes and faults. If you make a mistake, own it and learn from it.

Excuses are false reasons or inaccurate justifications used to absolve you of responsibility. However, the truth is they are nothing more than unproductive lies designed to protect your ego. They are inherently dangerous to both the athlete and warrior because they distort reality and prevent the practitioner from learning from his or her mistake. Excuses contradict and undermine the self-awareness required to achieve all forms of peak performance. Therefore, it's in your best interest to consider adopting a zero tolerance policy for excuses.

The Athlete's Responsibility

Regardless of the sport or activity, athletes have a broad range of responsibilities. Some include the following:

- Training (i.e., skill development, conditioning, nutrition and supplementation, proper sleep, etc).
- Attitudes toward the game.
- Attitudes towards teammates, coaches and spectators.
- Attitudes towards the opponent(s).
- Physical actions made during competition.
- Decisions made during competition.
- Arousal control during competition.
- Situational awareness during competition.
- Self-awareness before, during, and after competition.
- Evaluations or appraisals made after your   performance.
- Conduct and behavior off the playing field (i.e., acting as a positive role model for others to emulate).

A Soldier's Responsibility

A professional soldier is responsible for a wide range of individual duties and tasks. However, his most important responsibility is to his platoon. Early on, soldiers are taught essential team building skills that instill the critical importance of watching each other's back. While motion pictures portray Rambo surviving insurmountable odds on his own, the fact is a soldier will always be stronger and stand a greater chance of survival if he is part of a mutually supportive team. In short, team responsibility improves morale, group confidence, and overall military performance.

King Leonidas and his 300 Spartans

A good example of team responsibility can be found in the ancient Greek military formation known as the Phalanx. Perhaps you've seen it demonstrated in the action movie 300, where King Leonidas of Sparta and his 300 Spartans fought against thousands of Persians at the Battle of Thermopylae. Essentially, the phalanx was a cohesive rectangular military formation, consisting of heavy infantry armed with pikes, spears, shields, and similar weapons.

Foot soldiers (called hoplites) were organized into rows, typically about eight ranks deep, and stretching as far as a quarter mile long. Each hoplite carried a large round shield called a hoplon which protected his left side, as well as the man standing to his left. Hoplites would lock their shields together and form a massive wall of spears projecting toward the enemy. The phalanx would then slowly advance to ensure that it would not disturb its formation.

The military strategy of the phalanx formation was if individual foot soldiers stayed in tight formation and acted as a unified group, they could dominate their enemy. It was a team effort that required each foot soldier to trust his life to the man standing next to him. As a military formation, the phalanx was practically unstoppable. It functioned as a slow moving battering ram, designed for direct, bloody combat.

So what does an ancient Greek military formation have to do with teamwork? Actually, a lot! For the phalanx to be successful, it required each Greek hoplite to stand side-by-side with the next foot soldier, to create a densely packed formation. Each man had to trust his life to the man standing next to him. It was this team responsibility that ensured the success of the phalanx and the ultimate survival of the soldiers.

Courage

"Courage, above all things, is the first quality of a warrior."

-*Carl von Clausewitz*

Courage is at the essential core of any hero. Courage both inspires and validates the warrior. In all times and in all places, courage has been admired and revered, and has become the reason and the rationale for a society's success. But precisely what is courage? In many ways, it is easier to say what courage is not. Courage is not recklessness or foolish risk-taking, nor is it haphazard rage and fury. Instead, courage breeds confidence, resolution, and bravery. As many a fighter will tell you, fear can be intimately entwined with courage. Fear is the stimulus that, biologically speaking, triggers the fight-or-flight response; yet courage is choosing to stay and fight rather than to run away.

Courage Requires Fear

Courage is not the absence of fear, rather it's the ability to perform difficult actions or tasks when you are frightened. It requires you to confront a host of negative emotions and sensations including fear, anxiety, pain, intimidation, and trepidation. As you can imagine, courage is an essential quality for both warriors and athletes.

However, acts of courage are not just limited to elite soldiers or world-class athletes. In fact, everyday living requires courage. Often courage is demonstrated by ordinary people from all walks of life. Take, for example, something as seemingly trivial as a small and insecure teenager confronting an intimidating bully at school or an awkward and unpopular boy asking a girl out on a date. Although small by comparison with major acts of heroism, these trivial actions can be extremely stressful because they require taking action in the face of fear, apprehension, and insecurity. Most importantly, these small acts of courage are critical because they serve as steppingstones to greater acts of courage in the future.

The Coward and the Hero

Both heroes and cowards alike experience fear. However, the difference between the two is how each one handles it. When a coward experiences fear he will either freeze in his tracks or try to escape from the threat or danger. Conversely, when a hero experiences fear, he confronts it head-on by taking positive actions to overcome the obstacle or challenge.

What is Fear?

Understanding fear and it's effects on your mind and body is the first step to managing it. Essentially, fear is a strong and unpleasant emotional reaction to a real or perceived threat. If uncontrolled, fear leads to panic. Then it's too late to adequately perform.

The Three Levels of Fear

To prevent the negative effects of fear, you need to understand its levels and dynamics. For analysis, I have categorized fear into three different levels, listed in order of intensity:

1. **Fright** - quick or sudden fear.

2. **Panic**- overpowering fear.

3. **Terror** - crippling or immobilizing fear.

While these three levels of fear vary in degrees of stress, they all have one common root response: the fight-or-flight response.

What is The Fight-or-Flight Response?

Whenever a person, or any animal for that matter, feels threatened or frightened, certain physiological changes occur. They start in the brain when the hypothalamus sends strong impulses to the pituitary gland, causing it to release a hormone (ACTH) that stimulates the adrenal glands to release other hormones into the bloodstream.

Ultimately every nerve and muscle is involved. This adrenaline will cause an increased heart rate with a corresponding increase in respiration and blood pressure. Your muscles will tense up, you will start to sweat, and your mouth will go dry. In addition, your digestive system will shut down to allow a better supply of blood to the muscles. Your hair will stand on end (piloerection). Your pupils will enlarge so that your vision can improve. Your hand and limbs will also begin to tremble. Once these biochemical mechanisms and processes are fully engaged - and it takes only nanoseconds - your body will be in the fight-or-flight mode.

Arousal Control

For most people, the fight-or-flight response has a debilitating effect. They panic or freeze up, and fear then becomes a powerful weapon of the opponent. Therefore, it is critically important that you learn to control the physiological and psychological response to make it work for you and not against you in a critical situation. This is referred to as "arousal control."

The first step to controlling arousal is to accept the fact that the fight-or-flight response is a natural human response. In fact, it's one of Mother Nature's best ways of helping you survive a stressful situation. You've got to take advantage of this assistance by using the energy of the adrenaline surge to augment your physical performance.

Second, harness the fight-or-flight response by preparing yourself thoroughly for the danger that may one day confront you. Developing the psychological and physical skills of your craft will lead to a personal self-confidence. In turn, this confidence leads to an inner calm. Inner calm is the environment necessary for peak performance.

Third, actively employ coping techniques like meditation, mental visualization, positive self-talk, and controlled breathing skills to manage the immediate effects of stress, anxiety, and fear (much more will be discussed in chapter 6).

Fourth, develop a keen sense of self-awareness. Never stop assessing your state of mind and reactions to different stressful situations. For example, the next time you are startled by something, pay close attention. What was it that startled you and why? Did you freeze up? What did you see? What did you hear? Were you trembling and breathing heavily? Was your mind clear or distracted? Exactly what were you thinking about? How much detail can you remember? Did you make any tactical errors in your responses? These are only a few of the questions you should answer over and over again as you go through the process of preparing yourself psychologically.

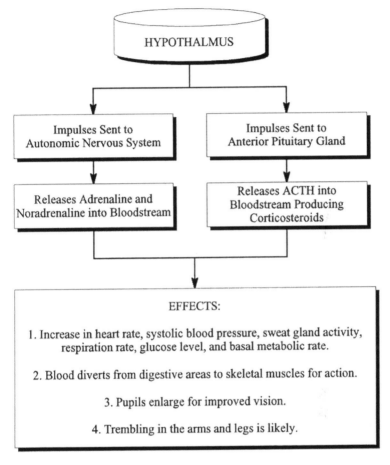

Another method of psychological preparation is written analysis. For example, write down five different hypothetical scenarios that truly frighten you. These scenarios could take place anywhere. Be specific with your details. Make certain to include the following relevant factors:

1. The source of danger and threat.

2. The time of day.

3. The environment.

4. Your mental, physical and emotional state during the crisis.

4. Any other relevant factors to your scenario.

Once you've completed these scenarios, have your coach or instructor identify the specific factors that elicit reasonable fear and then adjust your training to meet your concerns.

Possible Physiological Responses To Fear

1. Enlarged pupils

2. Dry mouth

3. Trembling hands

4. Cold, clammy hands

5. Increased heart rate

6. Shutdown of digestive system

7. Tense muscles

8. Sudden adrenaline surge

9. Hair stands on end

10. Enhanced alertness

How to Develop Courage

Courage is a tool that enables you to confront the fear. Like any tool, it can be developed and sharpened, so you'll be adequately prepared to deal with life's obstacles. When properly developed, courage gives you strength and empowerment to achieve your goal. It affords you the mental composure to perform risky and perhaps dangerous tasks with dignity and grace. Developing courage is a process that takes time. The goal is to take small steps that will progressively lead to significant acts of courage. What follows are a few guidelines to help you develop courage.

1. First, understand that courage is not the absence of fear. It is action made in the face of fear.

2. Realize that courage is critical to your survival. Intellectualize the alternative - living a fearful life!

3. Make it a habit to listen to or read the daily news. Pay attention to all stories relating to acts of bravery and heroism.

4. If you ever have the opportunity, talk to military veterans, law enforcement officers, firefighters, and other types of emergency responders. Their real-life stories are truly inspiring and often filled with acts of courage.

5. Get into the habit of stepping out of your personal comfort zone. Do things that you wouldn't normally do. For example, if you are a shy person, make a daily goal to initiate a friendly conversation with a stranger. Or ask someone out on a date. Remember, the goal is to take baby steps that will progressively build up your courage.

6. If you are someone who plays role-playing video games, consider only playing "permanent death" or dead-is-dead versions of the game. While this might seem trivial to non-gamers, the consequences are huge for people who invest hundreds of hours of their lives playing a game. Playing dead-is-dead, compared to just reloading a saved game, brings an entirely new dimension to gaming. Every action has tremendous repercussions for the player. It's not unusual for many gamers who play dead-is-dead to experience intense emotions such as stress, anxiety, apprehension, and even trepidation.

7. Learn how to mask your fear. Masking is the process of "staying cool" and concealing your emotions from your opponent when you are experiencing fear or trepidation.

It is the process of manipulating and managing your body language (both facial expressions and body gestures). In many cases, displaying signs of fear, anger, trepidation or weariness will just fuel your opponent's fire. Unfortunately, masking cannot hide some involuntary physical reactions (i.e., excessive perspiring, heavy breathing, trembling hands, etc.). However, the good news is you can cover them up by quickly moving about, diverting the opponent's attention elsewhere, etc.

8. Regularly use coping techniques like meditation, mental visualization, positive self-talk, and controlled breathing skills to manage your fears.

9. Depending on your situation, you can use scenario-based training and other stress inoculation techniques to manage fear.

10. Strive to master the knowledge, skills and attitudes of your craft.

11. Understand and accept the physiological responses to the fight-or-flight response.

12. Evaluate your past responses to crisis situations. What did you do right? What did you do wrong?

Chapter Four
The Steps to Mental Toughness

"No one saves us but ourselves. No one can and no one may. We ourselves must walk the path."

-Buddha

How to Develop Mental Toughness

Mental toughness is both a mindset and skill that can be developed with proper training. However, before delving into the specifics of training, it's essential that you first begin by identifying and defining your goals.

The First Step

Now is the time to sit down and identify exactly what you want. What do you hope to accomplish by training for the next 12 months? Your goal can be anything. For example, do you want to lose 20 pounds? Build up your self-confidence? Graduate from Navy SEAL BUD/S training? Win a sporting event? Or beat your PR (personal record) in the gym? Start now and write down all of the goals that you hope to achieve in the course of your training.

The Second Step

Once you have identified your goal, the next important step is to deconstruct and classify it into one of the following types of goal categories.

1. **Micro goal** - A micro goal is a long-term goal deconstructed into smaller task-specific objectives.

2. **Short-term goal** - Represents something you want to accomplish in a few hours or a day.

3. **Mid-term goal** - Represents something you want to achieve in a few days or a few weeks.

4. **Long-term goal** - Represents something you ultimately want to achieve in the future. Long-term goals often take months and even years to achieve. Examples might include winning a football championship, graduating college, becoming a Navy SEAL, owning your own business, etc.

For example, let's say your goal is to write a four-hundred-page novel, an arduous task that will take a considerable amount of time and effort to complete. However, if you break it down into small attainable goals, it can be accomplished. Instead of looking at the entire long-term goal of writing a novel, you break your goals down into smaller, achievable chunks such as chapters, pages, and paragraphs.

In this instance, maybe your micro goal would be to write three paragraphs today, followed by writing five pages tomorrow, and a chapter by the end of the week. It's this type of incremental micro-goal approach that will motivate and inspire you to stick with your goal and ultimately achieve your long term objective.

The Third Step

Once you have identified a very specific goal and have broken it down into micro-goals, the next step is to commit yourself to it. Remember, goals are useless unless you put them into action. Every day, you've got to set aside some time from your busy schedule to actively pursue these micro-goals. There simply is no way around it. The good news is, the more you hold yourself to these small goals, the closer you'll get to realize your long term objective. Moreover, you'll improve both your self-discipline and self-confidence at the same time.

One of the best ways to stay on track is to remind yourself constantly of your goals. Get into the habit of posting your daily micro-goals in places where you are likely to see them. For example, post reminder notes in places like the bathroom mirror, on your refrigerator door, on your bedroom nightstand, and the edge of your computer's monitor. If you're more of a gadget type of person, there are dozens of reminder and to-do apps available for your computer, tablet, and smartphone. These simple yet effective reminders will keep you organized, motivated, and focused on your goals throughout the day.

Mental Toughness Training

To reap the full benefits of mental toughness training, you have to reproduce both physiological and psychological stressors. Once again, your objective is to cope, perform and prevail from each stressful training event.

In addition, mental toughness exercises must be demanding and possibly lead to performance degradation. They must challenge and activate the individual building blocks of mental toughness.

Training simulations might not compare to actual life and death encounters or high-stress sporting events, but they come close. In fact, stress inoculation training is invaluable for developing the mental strength necessary to handle various types of stress. As a result, you'll experience less anxiety and fewer performance failures.

Finally, mental toughness training is not a substitute for skill development required by your particular sport, occupation, or discipline. It is supplemental to a foundational skill development program. However, if you have concerns about integrating mental toughness training with your current training program, consider talking with your trainer, coach, or instructor.

Physiological or Psychological Stressors

Stress and adversity come in many different forms. However, there are two broad categories of stressors: *physiological* or *psychological.*

A physiological stressor is something that puts strain on your body. It can be an injury, the sensation of pain, fatigue, or illness. A physiological stressor can also come from environmental factors such as sudden loud noises, poor lighting conditions, uneven or unstable terrain, extreme temperatures, etc.

In contrast, a psychological stressor is anything your brain interprets as harmful or threatening, and it can be caused by situations, events, circumstances, or individuals. Moreover, a psychological stressor can tax the cognitive and emotional systems of the brain.

Mental toughness exercises can also be used to test the strength and resilience of individuals. Pictured here, BUD/S (Basic Underwater Demolition/SEAL) Training at Naval Amphibious Base Coronado.

A beneficial mental toughness exercise should produce anyone of six types of stressors during the training event. They include:

1. Acute emotional stress

2. Mental confusion

3. Mental fatigue

4. Physical fatigue (muscular or aerobic)

5. Physical discomfort or pain

6. Environmental stress

Now that you understand the requirements for a mental toughness exercise, let's look at the different drills you'll be using in your program.

Scrimmages, Shootouts and War Games

Simulation training is ideal for developing mental toughness attributes, as well as sharpening specific physical and cognitive skills. The training objective is to replicate real-world experiences and events while protecting the participants from unnecessary risk and danger. Many different fields and disciplines use simulation training, including military, law enforcement, self-defense and sports.

Pictured here, U.S. Soldiers open fire on opposing forces during a battle simulation as part of a field training exercise at Saber Strike 2014.

Scrimmage Games

Every sport will have some form of competitive simulation training in their program. For example, football and hockey coaches will use scrimmage games to determine the value of their players. While, major league baseball has spring training to prepare players for the upcoming season and determine positions and active rosters.

Hogan's Alley

Police and law enforcement agencies regularly use simulation training. In fact, the FBI training academy has a 10-acre tactical training facility named Hogan's Alley, a realistic urban training environment for members of the FBI, DEA, and other local, state, and federal law enforcement agencies.

Hogan's Alley is an actual mock town that includes real life props, including homes, shops, a pool hall, post office, bank, hotel, and laundromat. The town is populated with actors who role play specific parts, including innocent civilians, terrorists, bank robbers, drug dealers, and other criminal characters. This unique training environment creates realistic and stressful simulations so that agents can learn a wide range of skills, including defensive tactics, firearms skills, and investigative techniques. Simulated munitions are also used to simulate gun fights with criminal characters.

Pictured here, a warning sign located at the entrance to Hogan's Alley at the FBI Academy in Quantico, Virginia.

The Killing House

Members of the armed services are frequently exposed to live fire training exercises in realistic combat environments. For example, the British Special Air Service (SAS) conducts hostage-rescue training in the "Killing House", a unique live-fire training environment designed to replicate a two-story building with four rooms on each level.

The primary objective of the Killing House is to train SAS operatives in the safest and most effective ways to conduct hostage rescue operations. A training exercise might include an SAS soldier playing the role of a hostage surrounded by cut-out figures of terrorist captors. The task of the SAS team is to make an explosive entry (using stun grenades) into the room, quickly assess the situation, and immediately neutralize the terrorist figures with live gunfire. The close-range firepower from the MP5 submachine guns along with real bullets flying in the air make this form of close-quarter battle training exceptionally realistic.

In this photo, U.S. Army Soldiers perform cordon and search exercises.

What's Next?

In the next chapter, I'm going to teach you a variety of mental toughness exercises that will help you achieve peak performance in all of your endeavors. They include both physical and cognitive drills that will expose you to many different types of stressors. Many of these exercises can be performed individually, while others will require the assistance of a training partner, instructor or coach.

A word of caution! Before you begin any exercise program, including the ones featured in this book, make certain that you have been cleared by your doctor.

Invincible

Chapter Five
Physical Training for Mental Toughness

"That which does not kill us makes us stronger."

- Friedrich Nietzsche

The Importance of Combat-Oriented Drills

The mental toughness exercises featured in this chapter were developed over the course of thirty plus years of teaching the combat sciences. You will discover that most of the drills and exercises are "combat-oriented." This is intentional for three principal reasons.

First, in order to adequately develop the mental toughness attributes, your training must be extremely intense and realistic. Compared to other forms of training, combat drills are the most demanding because they instantly create both physiological and psychological stressors. For instance, combat simulation exercises often present all six elements of extreme adversity, including danger, risk, fear, loss, pain, and self-confidence. In order for you to complete a combat-oriented drill, you must give it everything you've got!

Second, warriors who perform high-risk duties will find these drills invaluable for their occupations. Soldiers, law enforcement officers, security agents, and self-defense practitioners will acquire specific mental toughness attributes, while simultaneously developing life-saving fighting skills.

However, reality is the key ingredient, and you must always practice and train the way you want to react in a high-stress situation. In fact, I often tell my students, "train the way you want to fight and fight the way you train." In other words, you must methodically and safely integrate the frightening and spontaneous elements of fighting into your training program. Remember, under stress, you will instinctively revert to the way you have been trained.

For example, in my classes, I have students participate in dozens of scenario-based drills using a variety of equipment and environmental props. Since no two attacks are ever the same, I am constantly changing the combat scenarios in my program. When all is said and done, this realistic and dynamic form of stress inoculation training provides my students with the experience and confidence necessary to handle the volatile and unpredictable nature of combat.

In this photo, two soldiers engage in pugil stick fighting.

Third, athletes from all sports will benefit from combat-oriented drills. Regardless of your sport or level of play, these exercises will make you a much better athlete. It has been said that martial arts training is the foundation for all sports, and rightly so. The martial arts tap into every single physical attribute necessary for peak sports performance. Some attributes including: speed, quickness, power, coordination, agility, timing, aerobic conditioning, distancing, ambidexterity, endurance, flexibility, tactile sensitivity, kinesthetic perception, pain tolerance, awareness, finesse, accuracy, and non-telegraphic movement.

As a matter of fact, the NFL recognizes the importance of martial arts cross-training. For example, NFL teams such as the Dallas Cowboys, Kansas City Chiefs, Miami Dolphins, Green Bay Packers, and Denver Broncos have used martial arts training for skill development.

While the bayonet is seldom used on today's battlefield, it's an important tool for developing instrumental aggression in soldiers. In this photo, a Marine recruit goes through the bayonet assault training course at Parris Island, South Carolina.

Got Combat Skills?

You don't have to be a Navy SEAL, marine, martial artist or self-defense expert to perform many of the exercises featured in this book. However, there are some basic fighting skills you'll need to know if you want to get the most out of your training. Some skills include the fighting stance, kicking and punching techniques, and various defensive maneuvers.

For this purpose, I have included step-by-step instructions for performing these necessary skills. You can find them in the appendix of this book. Nevertheless, if you still need help with these foundational techniques, consider taking an introductory boxing, mixed martial arts or self-defense class.

Pictured here, two U.S. Marines practice ground fighting techniques in a martial arts program on Forward Operating Base Shir Ghazay, Helmand province, Afghanistan.

Warming Up

Before beginning any of the drills, it's important that you first warm up and stretch out. Warming up slowly increases the internal temperature of your body while stretching improves your workout performance, keeps you flexible, and helps reduce the possibility of an injury.

Invincible

Some of the best exercises for warming up are jumping jacks, rope skipping or a short jog before training. Another effective method of warming up your muscles is to perform light and easy movements with the weights.

When stretching out, keep in mind that all movements should be performed in a slow and controlled manner. Try to hold your stretch for a minimum of sixty seconds and avoid all bouncing movements. You should feel mild tension on the muscle that is being stretched. Remember to stay relaxed and focus on what you are doing. Here are seven stretches:

Neck stretch - from a comfortable standing position, slowly tilt your head to the right side of your neck, holding it for a count of twenty. Then tilt your head to the left side for approximately twenty seconds. Stretch each side of the neck at least three times.

Triceps stretch - from a standing position, keep your knees slightly bent, extend your right arm overhead, hold the elbow of your right arm with your left hand, and slowly pull your right elbow to the left. Keep your hips straight as you stretch your triceps gently for thirty seconds. Repeat this stretch for the other arm.

Hamstring stretch - from a seated position on the floor, extend your right leg in front of you with your toe pointing to the ceiling. Place the sole of your left foot in the inside of your extended leg. Gently lean forward at the hips and stretch out the hamstrings of your right leg. Hold this position for a minimum of sixty seconds. Switch legs and repeat the stretch.

Spinal twist - from a seated position on the floor, extend your right leg in front of you. Raise your left leg and place it on the outside of your right leg. Place your right elbow on the outside of your left thigh. Stabilize your stretch with your elbow and twist your upper body and head to your left side. Breathe naturally and hold this stretch for a minimum of thirty seconds. Switch legs and repeat this stretch for the other side.

Quad stretch - assume a sitting position on the floor with your hamstrings folded and resting on top of your calves. Your toes should be pointed behind you, and your instep should be flush with the ground. Sit comfortably into the stretch and hold for a minimum of sixty seconds.

Prone stretch - lay on the ground with your back to the floor. Exhale as you straighten your arms and legs. Your fingers and toes should be stretching in opposite directions. Hold this stretch for thirty seconds.

Groin stretch - sit on the ground with the soles of your feet touching each other. Grab hold of your feet and slowly pull yourself forward until mild tension is felt in your groin region. Hold this position for a minimum of sixty seconds.

Physical Exercises for Mental Toughness

In this chapter, I'm going to teach you specific drills and exercises for developing mental toughness. Most of them are the culmination of years of research, analysis, and experimentation. I have used these exercises to teach thousands of students over the past three decades and I'm confident they will help you in your training. We will start with scenario-based training.

Scenario-Based Training

Scenario-based training uses scripts of real-world experiences to meet specific training objectives in an operational environment. This type of simulation training is ideal for developing mental toughness attributes, as well as sharpening specific physical and cognitive skills.

What follows are two scenario-based drills that I regularly use with my students. They are *de-escalation* and *tactical options training.*

De-escalation Drills

Full-contact de-escalation drills develop several mental toughness attributes, including instrumental aggression, assertiveness, self-confidence, situational and self-awareness, selective attention, concentration, and arousal control.

What is De-escalation?

De-escalation is the strategic process of diffusing a potentially violent confrontation. The goal is to eliminate the possibility of an agitated individual resorting to violence. De-escalation is a delicate mixture of science and art, psychology and warfare. It requires you to be in total control of yourself, both physically and emotionally in order to deal effectively with someone on the verge of losing control. Simply put, it is the art of "tactically calming" the aggressor.

As Real as it Gets!

Full-contact de-escalation training replicates the violence and danger of a real street confrontation. I have participated and instructed these mock scenarios for over thirty years, and I can tell you they are as real as it gets. The adrenaline dump created by de-escalation scenarios is almost identical to that of a real situation. In fact, most of my students have reported experiencing the very same anxiety, stress and fear of a real confrontation.

Full-contact de-escalation training requires a minimum of two people, however, advanced practitioners can participate in multiple attacker scenarios as well. When it comes to this type of exercise, safety is of paramount importance. Both you and your training partner must always wear protective gear (i.e. headgear, sparring gloves, mouthpiece, groin cup, etc).

This form of scenario-based training also requires both spontaneity and the element of the unknown. For example, during a typical scenario your partner will play the role of a very angry and hostile person. This requires him to act out using numerous signs of aggression, including yelling, swearing, threats, challenges, pacing back and forth, rapid forward movement, parental finger (pointing finger in chest or face), heavy breathing, clenched fists, taut neck, hunched shoulders, shoulder shifting, etc.

Next, you must attempt to diffuse his anger. This means using both verbal and nonverbal techniques to calm him down, while simultaneously employing physical safeguards. However, there's no guarantee that your de-escalation skills will work. There is always the possibility your training partner will attack no matter how skillful and sincere you are in your efforts to avoid violence. If your partner does decide to attack you, he must do so with 100% commitment.

There are an infinite number of de-escalation scenarios that you can practice. The following will get you started.

SCENARIO 1: You are in a crowded bar having a good time. As you turn around to move to the other side of the room, you accidentally spill your drink on a patron's shirt. He becomes angry and begins to yell at you for being so clumsy.

SCENARIO 2: You are hurriedly driving down the road, and you accidentally cut off another motorist. As you walk into the grocery store, you notice the presence of the same motorist. Angrily, he starts walking toward you.

SCENARIO 3: You are walking down a city street with your spouse when a vagrant suddenly approaches you, asking for money. You reply that you don't have anything to give him. He becomes angry and begins to yell obscenities at the both of you. De-escalate the situation.

SCENARIO 4: You are walking your date to her front door when suddenly you are confronted with her angry and jealous ex-boyfriend.

SCENARIO 5: You and your friend are watching a movie in a crowded theater. The two people in front of you continue to talk throughout the picture. You politely ask them to be quiet. The man turns around and tells you to shut up. You respond by telling him to keep his voice down. The man stands up and angrily invites you outside.

SCENARIO 6: You are at a party. One of your best friends is drunk and becomes a nuisance to everyone. He approaches you and mentions how he envies you. Within a few seconds, his admiration turns to jealousy and anger. He says that you are spoiled and disloyal. He pushes your shoulder in an attempt to provoke you to fight.

SCENARIO 7: Your close friend is extremely drunk and insists that he is capable of driving himself home. To prevent him from driving, you grab his car keys and put them in your pocket. He is angry and embarrassed that you have taken his keys and demands that you give them back.

SCENARIO 8: You are driving through a residential neighborhood when suddenly a dog runs in front of your car. You immediately hit your brakes and get out to see what has happened. You notice that the dog is dead. A few seconds later, the owner of the dog arrives at the scene. She is hysterical and begins to scream at you for being so reckless.

SCENARIO 9: You have just pulled into a parking space at the shopping mall. As you open your car door, you accidentally slam it into the car parked next to you. The owner of the car gets out and begins to scream at you.

SCENARIO 10: You are at the beach, playing catch with your friend. As the ball is thrown to you, it accidentally lands in a sunbather's face. He jumps up and begins to threaten you.

Tactical Options Training

Tactical options training develops all ten building blocks of mental toughness, including instrumental aggression, assertiveness, resilience, self-confidence, self-discipline, situational and self-awareness, selective attention, concentration, philosophical resolution, responsibility and arousal control.

Tactical options training first requires you to rapidly gather and analyze information and then accurately evaluating it in terms of threat and danger. In general, you can assess people, places, actions, and objects.

What are the Tactical Options?

Accurate assessment skills will permit you to choose the appropriate tactical option. There are five tactical options to any self-defense situation. They are listed here in order of increasing level of resistance.

1. **Comply** - means to obey the assailant's commands. For example, if you are held at gunpoint (out of disarming range) for the purpose of robbery, there is nothing to do but comply. Take out your wallet, take off your watch, hand over your car keys, do what you are told. Comply

2. **Escape** - or tactical retreat means to flee from the threat or danger safely and rapidly. For example, if you are being held hostage and your captor is distracted long enough for you to escape safely, then do it.

3. **De-escalate** - means the art and science of diffusing a hostile individual. Not every confrontation warrants fighting back. Often you will be able to use de-escalation skills to talk someone out of a possible violent encounter.

4. **Assert** -means standing up for you and your rights. Through

effective communication skills, you can thwart a person's efforts to intimidate, dominate, and control you.

5. **Fight back** - means using various physical and psychological tactics and techniques to stun, incapacitate, cripple or kill your attacker(s). For example, you're trapped in a dead-end alley by a knife-wielding psychotic who appears determined to butcher you. Your only option is to fight back!

These are just a few of the many possible examples of the five tactical responses. Every self-defense situation is different, and, moreover, most situations can be fluid. A dangerous situation might present an escape option at one moment but quickly turn into a fight-back situation at the next. For example, let's say you are kidnapped, and your captor leaves a door unlocked, and in your effort to escape, you run into him on your way out. Obviously, that is the time to fight for your life.

How Does it Work?

Tactical options training replicates the stress and anxiety of a real crisis situation. This exercise requires a minimum of two people donned in protective gear (i.e. headgear, sparring gloves, mouthpiece, groin cup, etc.).

Tactical options training is similar to de-escalation scenarios. However, it differs because you have five options (comply, escape, de-escalate, assert, and fight back) to choose from, instead of just one.

This scenario-based training also requires both spontaneity and the element of the unknown. During a training scenario, your partner plays the role of any person and character he wishes. For example, he can be a concerned citizen, nosy next-door neighbor, an annoying coworker, intoxicated vagrant, arrogant classmate, enraged friend, etc.

Next, your training partner approaches you and initiate a

conversation that is relevant to his character. For example, if he's playing the role of the drunk, he might stumble about and ask you for money.

During the course of conversation, you must use your perception skills to assess the possible source of danger. In this case, what is this person's purpose in confronting you? Does he intend to rob you? Is he seeking retribution for something you may have done? Or is he simply looking to make some simple conversation with you? What is he saying and doing? How close is he? Where are his hands?

Pay very close attention to all available clues, especially nonverbal indicators. Your answers to these important questions will shape your overall tactical response. Let all of your five senses go to work to extract the necessary information. And don't forget to listen to what your instincts are telling you about this person.

Once you assess the situation promptly and accurately, you must reach a rational conclusion and choose the appropriate tactical response (i.e., comply, escape, de-escalate, assert or fight back). For instance, if your partner is acting like an irate motorist, your tactical option might be de-escation skills. Likewise, if he plays the role of an unarmed street attacker, you'll have to fight back to ensure your survival.

A word of caution! You must always be alert when participating in this exercise. Don't become complacent and comfortable. Never assume there is no danger! Remember, there is always the possibility your training partner will attack you!

Impact Training

Impact training is a series of physical exercises designed to condition your mind and body to withstand the trauma of strikes and blows. It's also effective for developing mental resilience, attention control, and self-confidence.

In unarmed combat, there are two types of striking impact: snapping and breaking. Snapping impact shocks the head or body but does not fully penetrate it. It's quick but lacks substantial follow-through. A snapping blow usually makes a brisk, sharp cracking sound when it connects with its target. In contrast, breaking impact shocks and moves the head or body. It can break or fracture bones easily because it follows through its target (approximately three inches). You must be physically and psychologically prepared to tolerate both types of impact.

Impact training requires both forms of impact to be administered to specific body parts, including the shoulders, back, chest, biceps, triceps, abdominals, thighs, and calves. Striking these targets will not cause severe or permanent injury. Never strike the face, neck, throat, solar plexus, spine, groin, or joints during impact training. These anatomical targets are very sensitive and cannot be conditioned to withstand deliberate impact. Striking these targets can cause severe and permanent injury. It is imperative that your training partner deliver accurate blows and avoid these targets during training.

For impact training, your training partner will need a pair of boxing gloves or focus mitts to deliver the blows. When you begin, have your partner start off slowly with light strikes to your muscle groups, alternating snapping and breaking blows. Always remember to exhale when the blow makes contact. Over time, your partner can increase the speed and force of the strikes. Be patient with each other. It will take time and some experimentation before you and your partner can correctly gauge the amount of power. Impact training sessions should last approximately five minutes and should be conducted at least twice a month.

Medicine Ball Drill

Medicine Ball training develops mental resilience, self-confidence, and attention control. When used properly, it also promotes proper breathing, physical endurance, and the ability to withstand powerful blows to the body.

One of the best ways to train with the medicine ball is to have a training partner repeatedly throw it into your stomach while you are either standing or lying down on your back. Remember to exhale and flex your abdominal muscles when the ball is forcefully thrown into your body.

A good workout would include a two minute round with one-minute rest period. Depending on your level of conditioning and specific training goals, you might do this for a total of 4 rounds. A word of caution, however, medicine ball training is hard on the body, so practice no more than two times per week. .

Full-Contact Sparring

Full-contact sparring is a practical method for developing instrumental aggression, attention control, self-confidence, immediate resilience, and arousal control. It also develops many physical attributes like speed, quickness, coordination, agility, timing, distancing, ambidexterity, endurance, flexibility, tactile sensitivity, pain tolerance, finesse, accuracy, and non-telegraphic movement.

Sparring skills require combining kicks and punches into fluid and logical combinations. Basic sparring sessions are conducted at a moderate and controlled pace. The good news is you can spar just about anywhere, such as a gym, basement, garage and even outdoors. However, before you begin training, you'll need protective head gear, 14 oz boxing gloves, and a mouth piece.

Depending on your level of conditioning, sparring rounds can range anywhere from one to five minutes. Each round is separated by either 30-second, one-minute or two-minute breaks. A good sparring session consists of at least five to eight rounds.

Since sparring workouts are structured around time, you will need a good workout timer. Most workout timers will allow you to adjust your round lengths anywhere from 30 seconds to 9 minutes. Rest periods can be changed from 30 seconds to 5 minutes depending on your level of conditioning and training goals.

When You Get Hit!

If and when you get hit in a sparring session, stay in control of your emotions and don't panic. Keep both hands up, stay mobile, and remain defensively alert. Maintain proper breathing, employ positive self-talk, and don't allow negative thoughts to contaminate your mind. Stay focused on the task at hand and continue to look for openings in your training partner's defenses.

Here are ten common mistakes that are made when sparring. Overcoming these errors will significantly enhance your mental toughness attributes.

1. Quitting or giving up after being hit.

2. Being distracted (internally or externally) when fighting.

3. Fearful or excessive blinking.

4. Randomly throwing punches or failing to focus on a particular target.

5. Lack of commitment when attacking your partner.

6. Hesitating or overthinking.

7. Turning your head away or closing your eyes when a blow is thrown at you.

8. Turning your body completely sideways from the sparring partner.

9. Running away from your opponent's attack.

10. Nervously swatting your sparring partner's boxing glove.

Handicapped Sparring

Handicapped sparring develops immediate resilience, self-confidence and arousal control while sharpening and refining individual fighting techniques. This form of restricted sparring is conducted by having one person spar with only one arm at a time. For example, during the course of a three-minute round, you are restricted to attacking and defending with only your right arm while your training partner can spar with both of his limbs.

Handicapped sparring can also include fighting opponents who are significantly larger than you. For example, see what it is like to spar someone who is two feet taller than you, or experience what it's like to exchange punches with someone who is 100 pounds heavier than you. These different types opponents will create the necessary mental and physical stressors to improve your mental toughness.

Hip Fusing Drill

Hip fusing is an advanced form of sparring that develops attention control, instrumental aggression, self-confidence, immediate resilience, and arousal control.

Hip fusing requires tethering yourself to your partner with a heavy-duty chain. To perform the hip fusing drill, place a weight lifting belt on each participant. Next, attach a heavy-duty chain (approximately 4 feet in length) to each belt. The length of the chain will depend on your skill level. For example, a longer chain would be used for beginners who need more defensive reaction time to defend against the blows.

A word of caution. Prematurely engaging in hip fusing drills can be dangerous and counterproductive. Remember, hip fusing is for advanced practitioners who have a solid foundation in full-contact sparring. Never participate in hip fusing until you have acquired the following skills:

1. A strong foundation in offense and defensive skills.

2. The ability to control the force of your offensive techniques.

3. The fundamental attributes of unarmed combat (i.e. speed, timing, coordination, accuracy, balance, and the ability not to telegraph your movements

4. A safe attitude toward training.

Circle Combat

Circle combat develops several mental toughness attributes, including self-confidence, immediate resilience, situational awareness, selective attention, and arousal control.

This drill is conducted by having approximately 5 participants form a large circle (approximately 12 feet in diameter) around one person standing in the center. All of the participants must wear protective gear.

The drill begins with the instructor randomly selecting participants from the circle to attack the person in the middle. The defender must immediately identify and react to the attack using various defensive skills and techniques. Once the attacker finishes his assault, he returns to the circle, and the instructor immediately calls out another attacker. Once the practitioners become familiar with this drill, the instructor can make it more difficult by speeding up the selection of attackers, calling out multiple attackers at once, incorporating bludgeon and knife attacks, and even having the attackers take the fight to the ground.

Circle combat can last anywhere from 30 seconds to 5 minutes. It's up to the coach and the student's level of conditioning.

The Three Training Methodologies

There are three specific training methodologies used to develop mental toughness, as well as the fundamental skills of armed and unarmed fighting. They are proficiency training, conditioning training, and street training.

Proficiency Training

Proficiency training develops important attributes like self-discipline, immediate resilience, and attention control. When conducted properly, it also develops speed, power, accuracy, non-telegraphic movement, balance, and psychomotor skills. The training objective is to sharpen one specific body weapon, maneuver, or technique at a time by executing it over and over for a prescribed number of repetitions. Each time the technique is executed with clean form at various speeds. Movements can also be performed with your eyes closed to develop a kinesthetic feel for the action.

Proficiency training can be accomplished through the use of various types of equipment, including the heavy bag, double-end bag, focus mitts, training knives, mock pistols, striking shields, shin and knee guards, foam and plastic bats, mannequin heads, and so on.

Conditioning Training

The next methodology is conditioning training, and it's used for developing self-confidence and immediate resilience. Conditioning training also develops endurance, fluidity, rhythm, distancing, timing, speed, footwork, and balance.

Conditioning training can be performed on various pieces of equipment, including the heavy bag, double-end bag, focus mitts, body opponent bag, and against imaginary assailants in shadow fighting.

In most cases, conditioning training requires the practitioner to deliver a variety of fighting combinations for three or four-minute rounds separated by 30-second breaks. Like proficiency training, this type of training can also be performed at various speeds. A good workout consists of at least five rounds. Conditioning training is not necessarily limited to just three or four-minute rounds. For example, in some of my classes, I will have advanced students ground fighting for 30 minutes or longer.

Street Training

Street training is primarily used for developing instrumental aggression. However, it also improves speed, power, explosiveness, target selection and recognition, timing, footwork, pacing, and breath control.

Street training prepares you for the sudden stress and immediate fatigue of a real fight. Since many violent altercations are explosive, lasting an average of twenty seconds, you must train for this possible scenario. This means delivering explosive and powerful compound attacks with vicious intent for approximately twenty seconds, resting one minute, and then repeating the process.

You should practice this training methodology in different

lighting, on different terrains, and in different environmental settings. You can use different types of training equipment as well. For example, you can prepare yourself for multiple assailants by having your training partners attack you with focus mitts from a variety of angles, ranges, and target postures. For twenty seconds, go after them with vicious low-line kicks, powerful punches, and devastating strikes.

Focus Mitt Training

Focus mitt training develops several mental toughness attributes, including instrumental aggression, resilience, self-confidence, awareness, and attention control. It also improves defensive skills, accuracy, speed, target recognition, target selection, target impact, and timing in all offensive techniques.

The focus mitt (also called punching mitt or focus pad) is an exceptional piece of training equipment that can be used by anyone. By placing the mitts at various angles and levels, you can perform every conceivable kick, punch, or strike known to mankind. Properly utilized, focus mitts will refine your defensive reaction time and condition your entire body for combat.

Focus mitts are constructed of durable leather designed to withstand tremendous punishment. Compared to other pieces of equipment, the focus mitt is relatively inexpensive. However, an effective workout requires two mitts (one for each hand). Your training partner (called the feeder) plays a vital role in focus mitt workouts by controlling the techniques you execute and the cadence of delivery. The intensity of your workouts will depend largely upon his or her ability to manipulate the mitts and push you to your limit. I often tell my students that a good focus mitt feeder is one step ahead of his training partner, whereas a great focus mitt feeder is two steps ahead of his partner.

When training with your partner, give them constructive feedback and let them know how he or she is doing. Remember, communication is vital during your workout sessions. Also, try to avoid remaining stationary. Get into the habit of constantly moving around with quick, economical steps.

To truly benefit from any focus mitt workout, you must learn to concentrate intensely throughout the entire session. You must block out both internal and external distractions. Try to visualize the focus mitt as a living, breathing assailant, not an inanimate target. This type of visualization will make the difference between a poor workout and a great training session. You also might want to draw small Xs on the mitts. This practice will improve your focus and concentration and help you develop accurate striking techniques.

All three training methodologies (proficiency training, conditioning training, and street training) can also be applied to the focus mitts. For example, if you applied the street training methodology you can prepare yourself for a ballistic street assault by having your training partner attack you with focus mitts from a variety of angles and ranges of combat. For twenty seconds, go after him with vicious and devastating strikes. Rest for one minute and then go again. The training possibilities are truly endless.

The Gauntlet Drill

The gauntlet drill builds instrumental aggression, mental resilience, attention control and situational awareness. To perform this exercise, you will need a minimum of ten people, each one holding a focus mitt. Divide the ten people into two equal rows and make certain they hold the glove at approximately head level.

Next, have the designated striker start from the top of the rows. From a fighting stance, have him deliver a lead straight/rear cross combination in a crisscross fashion while steadily moving down the two rows. Once he works his way through the "gauntlet," he should quickly return to the starting position (top of the row) and begins again. A good workout would be to perform this drill for 10 minutes non-stop.

Here, a student performs the strenuous gauntlet drill. Notice how close the feeders are to the striker.

Heavy Bag Training

Heavy bag training builds instrumental aggression, immediate resilience, self-confidence, and attention control. Heavy bag work is regularly used in boxing, kickboxing, mixed martial arts, and self-defense. It is also popular among people who just want to stay in shape or add a new dimension to their fitness programs. Many people use the heavy bag for some of the following reasons:

- It conditions the entire body.

- It improves muscular endurance.

- It strengthens bones, tendons, and ligaments.

- It conditions the cardiovascular system.

- It relieves stress and helps channel aggressive energy.

The heavy bag is constructed of either top grain leather, canvas or vinyl. Most bags are 14 inches in diameter and 42 inches in length. The interior of the bag is filled with either cotton fiber, thick foam, sand or other durable material. Depending on the brand, heavy bags can weigh anywhere from seventy-five to two hundred and fifty pounds. However, for our purposes, I suggest a bag that weighs a minimum of 150 pounds.

Safe and effective heavy bag training will require you to find a place that will allow both you and the bag to move around freely. The location should also be a relatively quiet place that is free of distractions. Here are a few places you might want to consider:

- Garage

- Carport

- Basement

- Barn

- Home gym (if you are fortunate enough)

- Open field or backyard

- Warehouse

- Under a deck

Before you begin working out, invest in a good pair of bag gloves that will protect your hands when working out. When buying gloves, spare no expense and look for a reputable and high-quality brand. This will provide years of reliable use and will help ensure a better quality workout.

If you don't think you'll need bag gloves, think again. Striking the heavy bag without hand protection causes sore knuckles, bruised bones, hand inflammation, sore wrists and scraped knuckles. As a result, it will set your training back for several weeks in order for your hands to heal.

A good heavy bag workout consists of at least five rounds lasting three minutes in duration. However, you can also apply the other two methodologies (proficiency and street training) to your routine. Here are some important tips when working out on the bag:

1. Always warm up with some light stretching and calisthenics before working out.

2. Gradually build up the force of your blows. Remember, a beginner's wrists are too weak to accommodate full-force punches.

3. Never sacrifice balance for power.

4. Remember to snap your punches.

5. Always keep your wrists straight when striking the bag.

6. Always maintain proper form.

7. Move around and avoid remaining stationary.

8. Learn to integrate your kicks, punches, and strikes into logical compound attacks.

9. Pace yourself to avoid premature exhaustion.

10. Don't wear jewelry or a watch when training.

11. Stay relaxed and avoid unnecessary muscular tension.

12. Never hold your breath. Remember to exhale with the delivery of each and every technique.

13. Avoid the urge to stop the bag from moving. Let it swing freely!

14. If you don't know the proper way to throw a punch or kick, get instruction from a qualified coach or instructor.

15. Avoid heavy bag training two days in a row. Give your body a few days to recover from your last workout.

The Elevation Drill

The elevation drill develops power punching skills while building instrumental aggression, mental resilience, and attention control. The objective of this exercise is to keep the heavy bag elevated at a

45-degree angle by continuously punching it. This drill is brutal on the arms. In fact, the average person can barely last 30 seconds. To perform the exercise follow these steps:

1. Face the heavy bag and assume a fighting stance.

2. Deliver the lead straight and rear cross combination continuously. Concentrate on delivering full-speed, full-force punches.

3. Maintain a rapid-fire cadence to keep the bag elevated at a 45-degree angle from the floor.

4. Avoid pushing the bag, remember to snap each blow.

5. Perform the drill for a total of 5 rounds. Each round should last anywhere from 30 to 60 seconds. If you are exceptionally conditioned, go for 90 seconds.

Here, a student performs the elevation drill.

The Pummel Drill

The pummel drill develops instrumental aggression, immediate resilience, and self-confidence. Pummeling requires you to attack a heavy bag or body opponent bag with a flurry of strikes from the top mounted position for specified period of time. To execute the pummel drill, apply the following steps:

1. Place a heavy bag on the floor.

2. Have your training partner tie a rope (approximately five feet long) to the top of the bag.

3. Mount the heavy bag (the same way you would mount an assailant in a ground fight).

4. For 30 seconds employ full-speed, full-force strikes on the upper portion of the heavy bag. Be vicious and attack the back with all of the aggression you can muster. There are two punches that can be delivered effectively from this position: linear punches and hammer fist strikes.

113

5. Have your training partner pull vigorously (side to side, and up and down) on the rope while you deliver the blows. Strive to maintain a good base and avoid losing your balance when your partner tugs the bag.

6. Rest for one minute, and then repeat the process for a total of ten sets.

The Head-Hunter Drill

The head-hunter drill is a spin-off from the street training methodology. It is designed to sharpen and develop hook punches while building instrumental aggression, mental resilience, attention control and situational awareness.

To perform the drill, assume a fighting stance and square off in front of a heavy bag or focus mitts. Next, execute a lead and rear hook combination (back and forth) with maximum power and speed for 30 seconds. Don't stop attacking your target until the time has elapsed. Rest for approximately 1 minute and then go again for five to ten rounds. Be forewarned! This drill is exhausting.

Shadow Fighting

Shadow fighting is the creative deployment of offensive and defensive techniques against imaginary assailants. It requires intense mental concentration, honest self-analysis, and a deep commitment to improving you fighting skills. Regular shadow fighting develops instrumental aggression, resilience, self-confidence, and attention control.

For someone on a tight budget, the good news is that shadow fighting is inexpensive. All you need is a full-length mirror and a place to work out. The mirror is vital. It functions as a critic, your personal instructor. If you're honest, the mirror will be too. It will point out every mistake - telegraphing, sloppy footwork, poor body mechanics, and even lack of physical conditioning.

Proper shadow fighting also develops speed, power, balance, footwork, compound attack skills, sound form, and finesse. It even promotes a better understanding of the ranges of combat. As you progress, you can incorporate light dumbbells or a weight vest into shadow fighting workouts to enhance power and speed.

A good shadow fighting workout consists of at least five rounds lasting

three minutes in duration. Don't forget that you can also apply the proficiency and street training methodologies to your routine.

360-Degree Blocking Drill

The 360-degree blocking drill develops resilience, situational awareness, and attention control. To perform the exercise, apply the following steps:

1. Have your training partner stand approximately three feet from you.

2. Position yourself in a 45-degree fighting stance with both of your arms relaxed and hanging at your sides.

3. Without your partner telegraphing his intentions, have him deliver a random swing at your head or torso.

4. Immediately respond with the appropriate block.

5. Return your arm back to the starting position.

6. Have your partner immediately attack with another swing at a different angle.

As you become more proficient with this defensive drill, your training partner should deliver a sequence of random swings with greater speed and force. In addition, you can have your partner incorporate linear blows into the drill. Just remember to start out slowly and progressively build up the speed and force of your strikes.

Sidestepping Drill

The sidestepping drill improves both situational awareness and attention control. It also develops your sense of distance and timing. To practice the sidestepping exercise, employ the following:

1. Begin with your training partner standing approximately 10 feet from you.

2. Assume a fighting stance.

3. Without telegraphing his movement, your training partner should charge at you full speed.

4. If you're standing in a right stance, quickly step with your right foot to the right and have your left leg follow an equal distance.

5. When performed correctly, your partner should miss your body, and you should be in a balanced and ready position.

6. If your training partner runs into you, it's because you are moving too slowly. To remedy this problem, keep your weight evenly distributed and explode off the balls of your feet.

7. If your training partner tracks you, it's because you are moving too soon. To remedy this problem, avoid premature

movements and wait until the very last second before you explode laterally.

Finally, you can practice the sidestepping drill with different stances, at various distances, in different lighting conditions, and while wearing a weight vest.

Disability Training

Disability training develops immediate resilience, situational awareness, and attention control. The goal is to experience what it's like to fight when you are under the weather or temporarily handicapped. Here are a few suggestions that will help get you started.

1. Practice shadow fighting when you're plagued with a migraine headache.

2. Practice close-quarter fighting techniques when confined to a wheelchair.

3. Spar with one arm in a sling.

4. Practice blocking and parrying skills while standing on crutches.

5. Perform proficiency training on the heavy bag when you have the flu.

6. Perform endurance push ups when you have a bad cough.

7. Ground fighting when you are feeling fatigued or exhausted.

8. Perform the circle combat drill when you are suffering from a hangover.

9. Practice escaping from grabs, chokes, locks, and holds while you are blindfolded.

10. Spar while wearing a weight vest.

11. Wear an elevation training mask when working out on the

heavy bag.

12. Want to experience some real physical discomfort, try sparring with a marble in your shoe.

Adverse Weather & Unstable Terrain Training

Training outdoors in adverse weather conditions and working out on different types of unstable terrain will also build mental toughness. Here are a few suggestions:

1. Perform endurance push-ups in the rain.

2. Work out on the focus mitts without gloves during the freezing winter temperatures.

3. Execute compound attacks in hot, humid summer weather.

4. Conduct shadow fighting in the snow or mud.

5. Spar when it's foggy outside.

6. Practice kicking techniques in gusty winds.

7. Grapple and ground fight in the dark.

8. Practice knife defense skills in poor lighting conditions.

9. Try speed-loading your gun when your hands are wet from rain.

10. Perform gun disarming skills with the sun in your eyes.

Unstable Terrain

1. Try sparring in tall grass.

2. Try focus mitt training on the ice (be careful).

3. Perform kicking techniques on wet pavement or grass.

4. Ground fight in the heavy wet snow.

5. Practice the sidestepping drill on gravel or mud.

6. Practice hip fusing in the sand.

Weight Vest Training

Weight vest training is unmatched for developing mental resilience. However, in order to get the best results from your workout, you'll need to invest in a high-quality vest that provides both comfort and durability. The vest must also be able to support a significant amount of weight, ranging anywhere from 50-150 pounds.

While there are countless high-intensity-short-duration workouts that can be performed with a weight vest, mental toughness training requires moderate intensity long duration workouts. Weight vest training for mental toughness resiliency has only three requirements:

1. You must carry enough weight to create immediate and significant stress on your body.

2. The physical stress and strain must be continuous and uninterrupted.

3. The workout session should be performed for a prolonged period, ranging anywhere from 45 to 60 minutes in duration.

One of the best ways to achieve these requirements is by taking extended walks in various types of environments. For example, try walking or hiking with a 75-pound vest for a duration of one hour. This may sound easy to some athletes, but I assure you that it is not. This type of workout is grueling and draining on both the mind and body.

If possible, train outdoors, instead of using a treadmill. While the treadmill does have some advantages, (i.e., when weather conditions are dangerous, or when training outside isn't an option, etc.) it can also be detrimental to your mental toughness training.

Working out on a treadmill always gives you the option of ending your workout prematurely. For example, if you get tired because you bit off more than you can chew, you can always hit the stop button and take off the vest. Knowing this simple fact creates a psychological comfort zone that makes the activity less daunting.

On the other hand, outdoor training is more unsettling. You are exposed to the elements, extreme temperatures, and unpredictable terrain. Most importantly, outdoor training doesn't provide you with the luxury of quitting prematurely. You don't have the option of stopping and taking off your vest. In essence, you must finish what you started.

A word of caution. Weight vest training is extremely demanding on the body. Be very careful when starting out. Always begin with a small amount of weight and progressively add more over time. Never train with a lot of weight. Remember, your body needs time to adapt to the weight. Finally, be certain to speak to your doctor first to see if you have any condition that might be aggravated by this type of training.

Physical Fitness & Nutrition

There is no escaping the fact that the human mind and body are intrinsically linked to one another. Mental toughness requires that your mind and body work harmoniously together as a single well-oiled machine. All of its components must work efficiently and synchronize properly if you want to achieve optimal performance in any endeavor. Real mental toughness is both a combination of mental conditioning and physical fitness.

No one can argue with the fact that most high-risk occupations are mentally and physically demanding. Moreover, many violent situations are unpredictable and occur without warning. Warriors must be able to handle the sudden and intense demands placed on the body during a crisis. Physical fitness or combat conditioning is the best way to achieve this goal.

Physical fitness is also critical for sports performance. Besides sport specific training, athletes also need to be physically fit. A physically fit athlete is more likely to reach his or her full potential. In most cases, they perform more efficiently and effectively and are less likely to be injured. Finally, athletes who regularly work out are more disciplined and possess greater self-confidence than their unconditioned counterparts

Fitness and Combat Conditioning

If warriors and athletes want to achieve peak performance, they must be physically fit. It's that simple. Fitness and conditioning comprises the following three broad components: cardiorespiratory conditioning, muscular/skeletal conditioning, and proper body composition.

The cardiorespiratory system includes the heart, lungs, and circulatory system, which undergo tremendous stress in a high-risk situation. So you're going to have to run, jog, bike, swim, or skip rope to develop sound cardiorespiratory conditioning. Each aerobic workout should last a minimum of 30 minutes and be performed at least four times per week.

The second component of conditioning is muscular/skeletal conditioning. To strengthen your bones and muscles to withstand the rigors of both sport and combat performance, your training must include progressive resistance (weight training). You will also need a stretching program designed to loosen up every muscle group. Stretching on a regular basis will also increase the muscles' range of motion, improve circulation, reduce the possibility of injury and relieve daily stress.

The final component of conditioning is proper body composition: simply, the ratio of fat to lean body tissue. Your diet and training regimen will affect your level or percentage of body fat significantly. A sensible and consistent exercise program accompanied by a healthy and balanced diet will facilitate proper body composition.

Exercise and fitness is not limited to warriors and athletes. Anyone interested in improving their overall health should exercise on a consistent basis. In fact, there are many good reasons why you should exercise on a regular basis. Here are just a few:

1. To increase longevity.
2. To lose excess body weight, which can shorten life.
3. To improve your circulation.
4. To tone and firm muscles and acquire the physical proportions nature intended.
5. To relax from tensions causing undue fatigue and loss of sleep.
6. To stay mentally alert.
7. To improve your metabolism.
8. To improve your immune system.
9. To acquire a more positive outlook through the feeling of good health and well-being.
10. To help maintain a youthful appearance.
11. To get more enjoyment out of life.
12. To improve your memory.
13. To improved posture.
14. To improved self-confidence.
15. To improve sleep.
16. To generate creative thinking.

Nutrition & Supplements for Mental Toughness

One important yet frequently overlooked aspect of mental toughness training is diet and nutrition. In reality, a true diet refers to a lifestyle of eating right.

To begin, 55 percent of daily caloric intake should consist of complex carbohydrates. Carbohydrates, the body's primary source of energy, are found in vegetables, fruits, potatoes, pasta, and all grain products.

Next we have proteins, which are essential for muscle and tissue growth. Poultry, fish, and legumes are excellent sources of low-fat proteins. Since you are involved in peak performance, you will require a greater amount of protein than the average person. Generally speaking, you should consume 1-1.5 grams of protein per pound of lean mass.

Finally, unsaturated fats are vital to proper metabolic function and vitamin absorption and should make up 10 percent of your calories. Don't confuse unsaturated fats with their nasty relatives, saturated fats. Saturated fats, found in ice cream, chocolate, cakes, and so on, are a big NO! Forget them. They will only make you fat and sluggish. Look for natural unsaturated fats in such foods as nuts, seeds, and various grains.

Do not forget to drink plenty of water throughout the day. Water is essential nutrient and it plays a significant role in all bodily processes. Try to drink at least one gallon of water per day!

Vitamins

Nutritional supplements should also be taken to ensure that you are receiving all the necessary vitamins and minerals within your diet. A vitamin is any of various fat-soluble (stored in the body fat) or water-soluble (dissolve in water) organic substances essential for the growth and maintenance of the body.

While a well-balanced diet will ensure that you are taking in the necessary amounts of vitamins, deficiencies can still occur, and they can have a negative effect on your training and overall performance. Be certain to get the following vitamins within your daily diet.

- **Vitamin A** - this fat-soluble vitamin is important for normal cell growth and development. Vitamin A can be found in fish-liver oils, carrots, liver, fortified dairy products, and some yellow and dark green vegetables.

- **Vitamin D** - this fat-soluble vitamin helps build healthy bones and teeth, and it can be obtained from fortified milk, fish, and eggs, and by exposing your body to sunlight.

- **Vitamin E** - this fat-soluble vitamin is used to treat abnormalities of the muscles, red blood cells, liver, and brain. This vitamin can be found in seed oils, especially wheat germ oil, plant leaves, and milk.

- **Vitamin K** - this fat-soluble vitamin is important for blood clotting and preventing hemorrhaging. It can be found in fish oils, liver, egg yolks, tomatoes, and green, leafy vegetables.

- **Vitamin B1 (Thiamin)** - this water-soluble vitamin functions as a coenzyme and is necessary for carbohydrate metabolism and neural activity. Thiamin can be found in meat, yeast, and the bran coat of grains.

- **Vitamin B2 (Riboflavin)** - is the primary growth-promoting factor in the vitamin B complex. It can be found in milk, leafy vegetables, liver, nuts, brewer's yeast, meat, and egg yolks.

- **Niacin** - a component of the vitamin B complex used to treat and prevent pellagra (a disease that includes skin eruptions, nausea, vomiting, nervous system disturbances, and mental deterioration). Niacin can be found in meat, fish, poultry, wheat germ, dairy products, and yeast.

- **Vitamin C (Ascorbic Acid)** - this water-soluble vitamin prevents scurvy and a variety of dental problems. Vitamin C can be found in citrus fruits, tomatoes, turnips, sweet potatoes, potatoes, and leafy green vegetables.

Supplements

Look at any fitness magazine you'll see hundreds of advertisements for supplements claiming to make you bigger and stronger in the shortest amount of time. With so much on the market, it's hard to choose the best supplements for your conditioning program.

Throughout the years, I have discovered three supplements that are tried and true for gaining lean muscle mass and strength. They include: creatine, glutamine and whey protein. Let take a look at each one.

Creatine

Creatine is a fascinating supplement that can benefit anyone who wants to boost their strength and endurance and build lean muscle mass. Creatine is a tasteless and odorless, white powder that is relatively inexpensive. Creatine mimics some of the effects of anabolic steroids. While results will vary from person to person, it's not uncommon for some people to gain 5 to 10 pounds of lean muscle within a few weeks of intense weight training.

The best time to consume creatine is approximately 1/2 hour before weight training and then right after a workout. Also, be certain to drink plenty of water when taking creatine (at least eight-8 ounce glasses per day). Creatine needs water for cell volumization of the muscle.

Be careful when purchasing creatine. There are some

manufacturers who sell impure creatine that can be harmful to your body. Make certain you are ingesting 100% pure creatine. Demand to see the HPLC (high-performance liquid chromatography) test results from whomever you purchased your creatine from. If you purchase creatine that has a strange smell or is yellow in color, return it immediately to the place of purchase and get a full refund.

Glutamine

Next, is Glutamine. Essentially, glutamine is an amino acid produced in the body that plays a vital role in protein synthesis. Despite its abundance in the muscles, glutamine levels can become quickly depleted when your body undergoes intense training. As a matter of fact, studies show that it can take up to approximately six days for Glutamine levels to return to normal after intense weight training sessions. While dosages can often vary from person to person, most people should take 5 grams. It has also been stated that the best time to take glutamine is right before you go to sleep.

Whey Protein

Whey is a high quality protein that is loaded with all the essential amino acids. The benefit to whey protein is that it is rapidly digested and helps quickly repair your muscles following intense training.

As you can imagine, there are numerous brands of whey protein sold on the market at various prices. The good news is whey protein tastes decent and comes in a wide range of flavors, so you will most likely find something that agrees with your palette.

How Much Protein?

There is much debate on the subject of protein consumption for conditioning, muscular development and overall health. Generally speaking, the average healthy adult male should consume approximately 1-1.5 grams of protein per pound of body weight. For example, a 175 pound man would consume anywhere from 175 to 262 grams of protein per day. This 1-1.5 protein ratio will help with the following:

- Build muscle mass.

- Maintain muscle tone while losing fat.

- Increase strength.

- Improving both sports and combat performance.

Reality Based Self-Defense Training

As I mentioned in an earlier chapter, combat drills are the ideal vehicle for developing mental toughness skills. In fact, athletes and warriors should consider taking their mental toughness training one step further by seeking hands-on training from a qualified reality based self-defense (RBSD) instructor.

Finding a Good School

However, you must be very cautious when choosing a martial art or self-defense school; they don't all have the same objectives. Here are some important points to consider before selecting a reality based self-defense (RBSD) school for mental toughness training.

First, don't select a school because of its geographical proximity. You must always choose the school that best suits your needs. Don't let your laziness force you to sacrifice quality combat instruction. Also, don't choose a school because of its aesthetics. Just because a particular studio has a juice bar or fancy equipment doesn't guarantee quality instruction. Ironically, some of the best self-defense instruction can be provided in garages, basements, school gymnasiums, public parks, and college campuses.

Obviously, finding a good school won't be easy, so plan to devote some time to the task. You might try looking in the Yellow Pages, on-line, or asking a friend if he or she knows of any reputable places. Or you may consider calling your local police department for some suggestions. Universities and community colleges can sometimes be good places to look for quality self-defense instruction. With patience, research, and some common sense, you'll find a good one.

When you do visit a school, be certain to watch a few of the classes. Evaluate what you see before making a choice. Consider the following questions: Is the environment conducive to mental toughness training? Does the instructor offer stress inoculation training? What types of arousal control techniques does he teach? Is the class physically demanding? Are the combat drills practical and realistic? Are the skills and techniques uncomplicated? What type of training equipment do they use? After the class is over, ask a few students if they are satisfied with the classes.

Make certain the school is strictly devoted to the art and science of real world combat. It should also be eclectic, drawing from such fields as martial arts, criminal justice, military and police science, psychology, sociology, conflict management, histrionics, physics, kinesics, anatomy, physiology, kinesiology, and emergency medicine. Other factors to consider before selecting a RBSD school include:

1. What is the cost? Can you live with the financial terms?

2. Are private or semiprivate lessons offered?

3. Are questions permitted during class?

4. What components of mental toughness are taught in class?

5. Does the school stress range proficiency?

6. Does the school emphasize the legal ramifications of self-defense?

7. Are full-contact drills a regular part of the training

curriculum?

8. Are children and adults taught together in the same class?

9. Is weapon instruction (firearms, knives, impact tools, OC sprays, etc.) offered?

10. Are training materials (i.e., books, manuals, videos, etc.) available to the students?

11. How many times per week can you attend class?

Finding a Good Instructor

You must also consider the instructor's qualifications and experience. In fact, you should choose a self-defense instructor the very same way that you would choose a surgeon to perform a difficult operation.

Since there is no standardized requirement for teaching RBSD, you're going to have to find out as much as you can about the instructor. Don't hesitate to ask a few questions about his background and credentials. If he's legitimate, he will understand your concern. Here are the questions to get answers to when selecting a competent instructor:

1. How long has the instructor been studying RBSD?

2. How long has the instructor been teaching RBSD?

3. Exactly which aspects of self-defense is the instructor qualified to teach?

4. What agency, institution, or individual certified the instructor?

5. Is the instructor well known (locally or nationally) for his or her expertise?

6. Is the instructor articulate and knowledgeable about criminal violence?

7. Does the instructor practice what he or she preaches?

8. Does the instructor look the part? Is he or she in shape?

9. Does the instructor teach the military or law enforcement agencies?

10. Does the instructor teach self-defense for a living? Or is it a part-time job?

11. Does the instructor project a professional image?

12. Does the instructor answer all of your questions?

13. Does the instructor's attitude show patience and respect toward his students?

14. Does the instructor seem genuinely concerned about your needs, or is he shoving a contract in your face?

Enrolling in a good RBSD school is a worthwhile investment. Along with learning life-saving combat skills, you'll also acquire a variety of other personal attributes such as physical fitness, personal empowerment, and self-discipline. Mind-body-spirit unification, self-confidence, and emotional control are also common residuals of serious instruction. But most importantly, with good self-defense training you will acquire a renewed appreciation of mental toughness.

Chapter Six
Cognitive Training for Mental Toughness

"To the mind that is still, the whole universe surrenders."

- Lao Tzu

Cognitive Exercises for Mental Toughness

In this chapter, I will be teaching you several cognitive exercises to develop and improve your level of mental toughness. Some of these exercises can also be used as coping tools during the immediate stress and anxiety of a high-performance situation. Let's start with creative visualization.

Mental Visualization

Through years of research and training, I found mental visualization to be a fascinating subject. Briefly stated, visualization is the formation of mental images to bring about desired goals ranging anywhere from improved lifestyles and health to better job performance and athletic ability. Established research indicates that mental images cause brain activity identical to that produced by an actual experience. Even if the image is unrealistic or logically impossible, the body will still produce a response that stimulates every cell in the body. There is no doubt that visualization can significantly improve mental toughness. To truly reap the benefits, however, you must make certain that your images are clear and strong. In essence, you must feel, taste, smell, and here the visualized scenario.

Visualization for Mental Toughness

Visualization serves many purposes in mental toughness training. As a training aid, visualization improves concentration, selective attention, self-confidence, instrumental aggression and helps maintain motivation during grueling workouts.

In sports, practice and training will only take you so far. In order to maximize your athletic potential, you must learn to use the mind's eye to further enhance your skills and abilities. The same applies to combat performance during extremely dangerous and hostile encounters. For example, visualizing strategic solutions to various high-risk combat scenarios also enhances performance and reduces the possibility of making tactical mistakes.

How to do it

Visualization is a natural and relatively simple exercise. The good news is the more often you use it, the easier it becomes. Effective visualization requires a quiet place, free from distractions, for at least 20 minutes. Turn off your cell phone and tell your partner or roommates that you do not wish to be disturbed. It is vital that you have peace and quiet.

Every visualization session must be undertaken in a relaxed state, the preparatory state for visualization. To attain a state of relaxation, you must first sit in a chair or lie on a couch or bed. If sitting, make certain your back is straight, your arms are uncrossed, and your feet are both on the floor. If lying down, place your arms at your side. You may want to put a pillow under your head.

There are various relaxation exercises you can perform. One of the easiest to learn is the tensing – releasing method. To begin, close your eyes and begin to breathe slowly and deeply for approximately 2 minutes. The next step requires you to tense every muscle in your body all at once. Clench your fists and your feet. Tighten your jaw and facial muscles. Tense your shoulders, chest, back, legs, and buttocks. Hold the tension for approximately 10 seconds then in one concentrated effort, let go and allow the tension to flow out of your body.

Visualization Examples

In this section, I am going to show you how to use visualization techniques to improve specific aspects of mental toughness. Here are two examples of what you can do with mental imagery. Let's begin with improving your training performance.

Training Performance Visualization

Before visualizing your training event, you must first have a clear mental picture of yourself. Begin by closing your eyes and visualizing yourself in a relaxed and peaceful state. Visualize your physical characteristics. Imagine your face. Note your eyes, nose, mouth, and chin. Observe the length and color of your hair. Now, look at your torso and concentrate on your chest and shoulders. See the veins that run up and down your biceps, forearms, and hands. Focus on your quadriceps, hamstrings, calves, and feet. Concentrate on the clarity of the vision. It may be helpful to glance at a picture of yourself occasionally to get a clear image.

Now, visualize yourself in a very serious training environment, maybe at a nearby gym. Visualize your surroundings. For example, envision a large, dingy and well-equipped gym. Feel the dank air against your face, neck and arms. Smell the subtle odor of sweat as you walk past three athletes working out. Listen to the sound of iron plates crashing to the floor. Remember, mental imagery is not limited to the visual. Concentrate on crystallizing this entire scenario. This may require you to run it numerous times in your head to bring it into full focus.

Next, picture yourself performing various weight training exercises. For example, you are now going to perform heavy squats. Envision yourself confidently walk up to the squat rack and load six 45-pound plates on the Olympic bar. See yourself tighten a weight lifting belt around your waist as you approach the bar. Imagine resting the back of your shoulders under the bar while holding it in place with both of your hands. Picture a solid stance with your feet approximately shoulder width apart from each other. Feel the heaviness of the weight and the strain in your muscles as you lift the heavy bar from the rack. Now, visualize the perfect execution of a leg squat - head up, back straight, and your feet flush against the floor. Watch yourself breathe deeply as you slowly lower your body to the squat position. Imagine yourself exploding upward back to the starting position. Experience the sensation of pure confidence as you start another repetition. Continue this mental imagery for each and every repetition in your set.

Now, visualize how you feel after your leg workout. Imagine the distinct soreness in your leg muscles. Feel them cramp and ache from complete exhaustion. Picture how difficult it is to walk up a flight of stairs after training your legs. Experience that priceless feeling of accomplishment and achievement as you amble your way to your car.

Instrumental Aggression Visualization

This visualization scenario is going to focus on developing instrumental aggression for combat performance. Start by visualizing yourself in a dangerous environmental setting, maybe walking through an alley in some seedy part of town. Feel the cool night air rush your body. Envision the gloomy brick buildings that surround you. Smell the rotten garbage as you walk past the overloaded trash cans. Listen to the sound of cars driving in the distance, hear an alley cat cry from hunger.

Now, imagine a distant figure lurking in the shadows, slowly approaching you. Mentally conjure up a person, giving him strong physical characteristics. Make him dangerous and threatening – perhaps a tall and powerful mesomorph. Begin with his facial characteristics and visualize his entire body. Smell the repulsive stench that radiates from his unbathed body. Give this imaginary assailant a criminal motive and a voice to express it. Feel your heart accelerate and your adrenaline soar. Don't forget to visualize essential tactical factors, such as the opponent's range, positioning, weapon capability, and state of mind. Again, it might be necessary to run the scenario several times in your mind to crystallize the confrontation.

Next, visualize an extreme reversal in your mentality – the aggressive side of your temperament. Watch yourself transform into a calm and controlled warrior. You are dangerous, courageous, and free from distractions. Your mind is razor sharp and focused on the confrontation.

Visualize your chest cavity expand as oxygen fills your lungs. Hose like veins protrude from your temple, and your face begins to grin with anticipation. You are ready to fight! You assume a fighting stance, and the storm of destruction begins. See yourself move forward with a brutal and vicious compound attack. The fighting techniques you choose are entirely up to you; however, be certain that they accurately relate to the circumstance, environment, range, and targets presented by the imaginary assailant. During your attack, picture the opponents bone shatter as you deliver powerful blows. Listen to him groan in pain and whimper in agony. Finally, watch the adversary fall to the ground, incapacitated and harmless.

Try visualizing the scenario at different mental speeds. Experiment with different combative scenarios. Change the environment, circumstance, opponent, range, and level of use-of-force. Be creative; remember, no two self-defense altercations are going to be the same.

Meditation and Mental Toughness

Meditation is a technique whereby the practitioner achieves a state of deep physiological and mental repose. It has been used throughout the centuries by the Indian yogis, Taoists, Buddhists, and the mystics to achieve self-enlightenment. It wasn't until the 60s that Westerners recognize the value of meditation for reducing stress, muscle tension, pulse rate, high blood pressure, and other ailments.

Meditation serves several purposes in mental toughness training. It develops both self-discipline and self-awareness. Meditation also enhances concentration. Through its practice, you learn to eliminate both internal and external distractions from your mind. Believe it or not, meditation also cultivates characteristics of instrumental aggression. Through consistent practice, you can acquire an emotionless state of mind that is essential for high-risk combat operations. Meditation can also be used to clear the warrior's mind after a dangerous and stressful combat event. Stress and anxiety are replaced with inner peace, patience and a state of well-being.

How to do it

Effective meditation requires a quiet environment and freedom from distractions for at least 30 minutes. A quiet and comfortable room will suffice. There is no need to burn incense or decorate your room in an oriental motif. Just keep it plain and simple. Meditation can also be practiced outdoors, as long as the location is quiet and peaceful.

Posture is another important factor. You want to be as comfortable as possible when meditating. There are many different types of meditative postures. The most common is the seated, cross-legged position, where the legs are crossed with the feet under the thighs. The head is balanced and facing forward, the torso is erect, and the hands are placed on the knees. This is by far the most comfortable and unrestricted posture. I do not recommend lying down; you should not be so relaxed that the mind becomes unfocused.

Once you are in a comfortable position, close your eyes and begin to breathe slowly and deeply, in through your nose and out through your mouth. The goal is to relax. The next step is the most difficult. You want to eliminate any thoughts from your mind. The objective is to remain mentally void. Don't let your mind wander or visualize. You want to reach a state of "nothingness." If thoughts or images do enter your mind, don't concentrate on them. Just allow them to drift from your consciousness. Concentrating on "nothing" can be difficult and very frustrating. It becomes easier with constant practice, however. If your schedule permits, meditate every day. If your time is limited, three times a week will suffice. Make sure each session lasts at least 20 minutes.

Remember that results will not come overnight. Like any worthwhile endeavor, meditation requires practice and time.

Controlled Breathing

Controlled breathing is a very useful technique for managing the stress and anxiety associated with a variety of high-performance tasks. This form of tactical breathing can be used by warriors and athletes. However, it's especially helpful for arousal control during high-risk duties such as those found in military, law enforcement, and private security work.

All of us, at one time or another, have experienced the uncontrolled breathing pattern associated with fear or extreme stress. If you recall, it was loud, fast and shallow. Therefore, the objective of controlled breathing is to do the exact opposite. By employing slow and controlled breathing, you will be able to regain control of your emotional state. Deep and steady breathing quickly shifts your mind and body into a more relaxed state, so you can efficiently perform your task or mission during a crisis situation.

How to do it

Initially, controlled breathing should be practiced in a quiet place, free from distractions, for at least 15 minutes. It's best to practice while sitting in a chair or lying on a comfortable couch or bed. If sitting, make certain your back is straight, your arms are uncrossed, and your feet are both on the floor. If lying down, place your arms at your side. You may want to put a pillow under your head.

Next, close your eyes and relax your body. Begin by inhaling deeply and steadily for 4 seconds. Let your lungs fill and expand with air. Hold this for one second and then exhale steadily for 4 seconds. Allow all of the air to expel from your mouth. Repeat this process for a minimum of 15 minutes. Advanced practitioners can also incorporate controlled breathing exercises with mental visualization scenarios. The more you practice controlled breathing, the faster you'll be able to bring about its relaxation response.

Once you master the basics, you can practice controlled breathing during idle times. For example, when you are waiting in a long line or when you are stuck in a traffic jam. However, controlled breathing is best used before, during and after a high-pressure performance situation.

Positive Thinking & Self-Talk

Many people underestimate the power of positive thinking. As a matter of fact, research suggests numerous health benefits from positive and optimistic thinking. Some include:

- Increased longevity
- Greater resistance to illness
- Improved productivity
- Improved self-esteem
- Improved physical well-being
- Reduced risk of heart disease
- Greater coping skills during stressful events

Positive thinking is especially important for mental toughness.

In order to effectively overcome adversity, you must possess the self-confidence and personal belief that you can overcome any obstacle or hardship. However, don't confuse positive thinking with arrogance, self-delusion or blind hope. Positive thinking must be predicated on competency. You must, in fact, possess the actual skills and attributes necessary to address your adverse situation.

Positive Self-Talk

Positive thinking is the environment necessary for effective self-talk. Self-talk is the internal dialogue you have with yourself during a stressful performance situation, and it's based on your beliefs, assumptions, and individual perceptions. This internal dialogue is essential to identifying and solving problems during a performance event. In fact, positive self-talk during performance situations improves attention control and will help eliminate self-doubts and false assumptions, which can destroy peak performance.

Positive self-talk is a skill, and like any skill, it takes practice. Here are several techniques that will get you started in the right direction.

- Be self-aware and learn to catch yourself when you are thinking negatively.

- Whenever a negative self-statement is made, quickly replace it with a positive and optimistic one. For example, change "I suck!" to "I love this challenge."

- Interrupt negative self-talk with a positive visual image of yourself (i.e., completing the mission, scoring a touchdown, defeating the enemy, etc.).

- Regularly visualize yourself in positive and favorable situations.

- Intentionally use positive words in your inner dialogues, or when talking with other people.

- Approach every situation or circumstance with favorable expectations.

- Make it a habit to take control of stressful situations.

- Try to associate with people who are positive and upbeat.

Using Cue Words

A cue word is a unique word or personal statement that helps focus your attention on the execution of a skill, instead of its outcome. It is also a very effective thought-stopping technique for halting unwanted thoughts during a crisis. For example, since the brain can only focus on one thing at a time, concentrating on a specific cue word is a very effective way of taking your mind off negative thoughts during a performance event. Cue words, however, should be positive, personal and short. They can also include action statements or instructional phrases.

Sample Cue Words or Statements:

- *"Attack!"*

- *"Explode!"*

- *"Tough!"*

- *"Dominate!"*

- *"Shoot!"*

- *"Fight"*

- *"Focus!"*

- *"Relax!"*

- *"Hit!"*

- *"Punch!"*

- *"Move!"*

- *"Steady!"*

Invincible

- *"Power!"*
- *"Hold on!"*
- *"Swing!"*
- *"Jump!"*
- *"Faster!"*
- *"In Control!"*
- *"Ready, Set, Go!"*
- *"Eye on the Ball!"*
- *"Crush him!"*

Optical Illusion Exercises

The following exercises are designed to improve your selective attention and concentration skills. Each drawing is an optical illusion that presents one of two different perceptual images. The goal is to concentrate and focus exclusively on only one perceptual image for a specified period of time. Start off with 15 seconds and progressively work your way up to 5 minutes. Remember, if your attention breaks (and you see the other image), you must start over again. This may sound easy to some, but I assure you that it is not.

1. Beginner level - 15 seconds.

2. Intermediate level - 30 seconds.

3. Skilled level - 90 seconds.

4. Advanced level - 3 minutes.

5. Mental Mastery level - 5 minutes.

The Rubin Vase

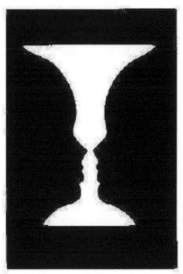

What do you see? Is it a curved vase or two faces looking directly at each other? Concentrate and focus on only one perceptual image.

Young Lady or Old Woman

What do you see? Is it a young lady or old woman? Concentrate and focus on only one perceptual image.

The Face

What do you see? Is it a woman standing next to a tree or a face staring at you? Concentrate and focus on only one perceptual image.

Woman Reading a Book or Old Man

What do you see? Is it a woman reading a book or the face of an old man? Concentrate and focus on only one perceptual image.

The Devil Face

What do you see? Is it a devil face or a group of women standing in front of their own reflections in a mirror? Concentrate and focus on only one perceptual image.

Bifurcation Training

Bifurcation training is ideal for improving selective attention and mental concentration. This exercise requires the practitioner to perform a particular physical performance action while simultaneously executing an unrelated mental task. The physical performance could be anything that involves technical skill and movement (i.e., a golf swing, tennis serve, baseball pitch, football forward pass, arrest and control maneuver, target practice, punching combination, etc). The mental task portion of the drill, however, requires you either to solve a mathematical equation or recite a verse or nursery rhyme.

Invincible

The following bifurcation drills will use a striking combination or "compound attack" as the physical performance action. Let's begin with the pledge drill.

Pledge Drill

This exercise requires that you verbally recite the pledge of allegiance. While you are reciting the pledge your training partner yells, "Go!" and you are to immediately launch a preselected compound attack in the air. The key is to deliver a flurry of full-speed, full-force strikes while continuing to recite the pledge in a calm and controlled manner. It's critical that you do not alter the tone, pitch, volume, or tempo of your voice when delivering your assault.

Nursery Rhyme Drill (beginner level)

This exercise is similar to "the pledge" except that it requires you to verbally recite a simple children's nursery rhyme, such as "Mary Had a Little Lamb" or "Hickory, Dickory, Dock." Once again, while you are reciting the rhyme, your training partner yells, "Go!" and you are to immediately launch a preselected compound attack in the air without disturbing the vocalization of the rhyme. Once again, it's critical not to alter the tonality of your voice when delivering your assault.

Tongue Twister (intermediate level)

The tongue twister is an intermediate-level drill that requires you to slowly and repeatedly recite a tongue twister, such as "She sells seashells on the seashore of Seychelles" or "Peter Piper picked a peck of pickled peppers." While you are reciting this statement, your training partner yells, "Go!" and you must immediately launch a preselected compound attack in the air. Once again, it's critical that you do not disturb the vocalization or alter the tone, pitch, volume, or tempo of your voice when delivering your assault.

146

The Alphabet Drill (advanced level)

The "alphabet" is a more advanced drill. Your objective here is to slowly recite the alphabet backward. At some point during your recitation, your training partner is to yell, "Go!" and you are to immediately launch a preselected compound attack in the air while continuing to recite the alphabet backward. Don't get frustrated with this exercise; it's designed to challenge you.

Sample Compound Attacks

What follows are five compound attacks that can be employed when conducting bifurcation training. A "compound attack" is the logical sequence of two or more techniques thrown in strategic succession. For example, a lead straight punch followed immediately by a rear cross is considered to be a compound attack. There are infinite fighting combinations you can perform during bifurcation training. (For more information about specific fighting techniques, please see the appendix of this book.)

When executing your compound attack, make certain your strikes are delivered with speed, power, and proper form. You can also perform these combinations in front of a mirror, on the heavy bag or the focus mitts.

1. Lead straight/rear cross/lead straight
2. Push kick/rear uppercut/lead uppercut/rear hook punch
3. Lead straight/rear cross/lead hook punch/rear hook punch
4. Hook kick/rear hook punch/lead hook punch/rear uppercut
5. Rear hook punch/lead uppercut/rear uppercut/lead hook punch

Opportunity Training

Opportunity training is used during idle times or when a unique situation presents the "opportunity" to practice your mental toughness skills. Here are a few examples:

Insomnia

All of us suffer from insomnia. Insomnia is generally caused by stress and anxiety from a variety of issues and factors, some include relationship and financial problems, job loss, moving, divorce, illness, emotional or physical discomfort, and environmental factors like noise, light, or extreme temperatures.

If you can't sleep, use it as an opportunity to work on your attention control skills. Practice controlled breathing and focus on blocking out the negative and stressful thoughts that are keeping you up. Continue doing this until you fall back asleep.

Delayed Trip

Imagine being stuck on an airplane for 6 hours on the runway. It sounds like hell, and it is. Use this situation as an opportunity to practice your mental visualization skills. For example, close your eyes and begin visualizing positive and vivid images, such as the plane taking off, the view from the window, the plane landing, and the feelings you will experience when you reach your destination. Keep visualizing these images until your plane actually takes off.

Crying Baby

Nothing claws at your brain more than a baby screaming on the top of his lungs. Instead of leaving the area, use this as an opportunity to develop your attention control skills. Try to filter out and ignore the high-pitch crying and blood-curdling screams. Direct your attention to something else in your immediate environment. For example, try memorizing lines of a verse during the tantrum. The turmoil around you can work to strengthen both your selective attention and concentration.

Tattoos

Getting tattooed is no picnic. As a matter of fact, it can be downright miserable. Especially, if you are having a lot of work done on a sensitive part of your body, such as the wrist, elbow or ribs.

Initially, getting tattooed might seem exciting, but I can assure you the excitement wears off real fast. The process of being tattooed is painful, boring and mentally draining. A few hours "in the chair" will make you want to scream and rip your hair out.

However, if you must get tattooed, use it as an opportunity to develop your mental resilience and attention control skills. Try to disassociate your mind from the constant pain and irritation of the needle digging relentlessly into your skin. Focus and direct your attention to something else in the room, perhaps a picture on the wall or an object on a table in front of you. Try to maintain this form of attention control for the duration of your tattoo session.

Reading and Research

The intellectual, or academic, aspects of mental toughness training cannot be overstated. You must possess an insatiable desire to learn and grow to your full potential. Academic research involves voracious reading. The body of printed materials on mental toughness has grown astronomically.

Try to read anything you can get your hands on. However, don't make the common mistake of passively reading material. Get into the habit of dissecting and noting literature. Strategically sound theories and unique training concepts should be noted and remembered. Books should be read over and over again until practical ideas are intellectually solidified. Finally, always read material with an open mind balanced with healthy skepticism.

Chapter Seven
Mental Toughness Programs

Creating a Solid Mental Toughness Program

We are now going to take all of the knowledge from the previous chapters and put it into action. In this section, I am going to show you how to design a mental toughness training program to suit your personal needs. However, before we begin, you must be certain that your program meets the following criteria.

- **Realistic** - your training should be as real as possible. It should include drills and exercises that replicate real world scenarios and conditions.

- **Simple** - your training should be easy to put into action. It should not require time-consuming preparation or expensive or complex equipment.

- **Specific** - your training should meet specific training goals. This might be a micro goal, such as improving your instrumental aggression during a particular scenario-based training drill. Avoid the urge to jump from one mental toughness attribute to the next. Instead, devote your attention to one skill at a time.

- **Stressful** - your training should produce one or more of the six types of stressors (i.e., acute emotional stress, mental confusion, mental fatigue, physical fatigue (muscular or aerobic), physical discomfort or pain, and environmental stress).

- **Quantifiable** - you must be able to accurately measure your progress in training. Performance measurement is motivational and helps you stay committed to your goals. It also useful for identifying methodologies that are not helping you reach your personal objectives.

Sample Mental Toughness Programs

Let me start by saying, there's no single mental toughness program that works for everyone. Since each of us has different goals, and timelines, it's up to you to identify your needs and personalize your training accordingly. The bottom line is, only you can determine what works best for you.

There are many ways to set up a mental toughness training program. In fact, some of you might want to first consult with your coach, trainer or instructor prior to setting up a program and schedule.

How to do it

What follows are several sample mental toughness programs utilizing both physical and cognitive exercises. Once again, these just serve as examples of what you can do.

STEP 1: IDENTIFY YOUR MICRO-GOAL: For this example, our immediate goal is to develop and improve the attention control attribute.

STEP 2: SELECT YOUR DRILLS: Now, choose from the list of drills that develop this particular mental toughness attribute. In this case, you will choose from the list below:

Physical Drills

- **Competitive event, scrimmage, or training simulation.**
- **De-escalation drills**
- **Tactical option response**
- **Impact training**
- **Medicine ball**
- **Proficiency training**

Invincible

- Hip fusing
- Gauntlet drill
- Sparring
- Handicapped sparring
- Circle combat
- Heavy bag training
- Elevation drill
- Head hunter drill
- Focus mitt work
- 360-degree blocking
- Sidestepping drill
- Shadow fighting
- Adverse weather training

Mental Drills

- Visualization
- Meditation
- Controlled breathing
- Bifurcation drills
- Optical illusion exercises
- Reading and research
- Opportunity training

STEP 3: DETERMINE YOUR TRAINING FREQUENCY:
Now, decide how many days per week your schedule permits you to train.

Example 1: Training five days per week

In this example, you will actively train five days per week.

MONDAY: • Meditation • Competitive practice event or training simulation
TUESDAY: • Visualization session • Controlled breathing exercises • Mental toughness reading & research
WEDNESDAY: (rest day)
THURSDAY: • Visualization session • Controlled breathing exercises • Full-contact sparring
FRIDAY: • Bifurcation training • Focus mitt drills • Meditation
SATURDAY: (rest day)
SUNDAY: • Meditation • De-escalation training • Gauntlet drill

Example 2: Training five consecutive days per week

In this example, you will train five consecutive days, followed by two days of rest.

MONDAY: • Visualization • Heavy bag training • Focus mitt drills
TUESDAY: • Meditation • Controlled breathing exercises • Optical Illusion exercises
WEDNESDAY: • Visualization • Competitive practice event or training simulation
THURSDAY: • Shadow fighting practice • Meditation • Controlled breathing exercises
FRIDAY: • Tactical options training • Bifurcation training • Meditation
SATURDAY: (rest day)
SUNDAY: (rest day)

Example 3: Training four days per week

This weekly program requires you to train four days per week.

MONDAY: • Controlled breathing exercises • Visualization • Meditation
TUESDAY: • Impact training • Shadow fighting • Elevation drill
WEDNESDAY: (rest day)
THURSDAY: • Competitive practice event or training simulation • Meditation • Controlled breathing exercises • Opportunity training
FRIDAY: • Proficiency training • Hip fusing • Visualization
SATURDAY: (rest day)
SUNDAY: (rest day)

Example 4: Training three days per week

This weekly program is a bit more conservative, it requires you to train three days per week.

MONDAY:
• Competitive practice event or training simulation • Visualization • Controlled breathing exercises
TUESDAY: (rest day)
WEDNESDAY: • Sparring • Medicine ball training • Controlled breathing exercises
THURSDAY: (rest day)
FRIDAY: • Head hunter drill • 360-degree blocking • Shadow fighting • Meditation
SATURDAY: (rest day)
SUNDAY: (rest day)

Example 5: Training cognitive exercises only

This program requires you to practice cognitive exercises exclusively. This form of training is helpful for individuals who are unable to physically workout because of a training injury.

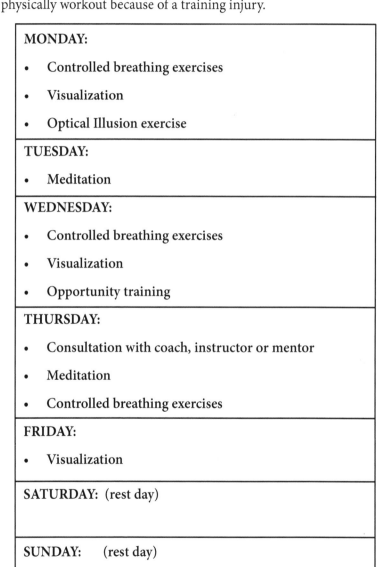

MONDAY:

- Controlled breathing exercises

- Visualization

- Optical Illusion exercise

TUESDAY:

- Meditation

WEDNESDAY:

- Controlled breathing exercises

- Visualization

- Opportunity training

THURSDAY:

- Consultation with coach, instructor or mentor

- Meditation

- Controlled breathing exercises

FRIDAY:

- Visualization

SATURDAY: (rest day)

SUNDAY: (rest day)

Mental Toughness Program Tips

- Commit yourself to only one mental attribute at a time. Devote a least one month to each micro-goal before moving on to another attribute.

- Try to participate in at least one competitive event/simulation training event per week.

- Try to get at least two visualization and meditation sessions per week. If you can do more, even better.

- Don't forget to use "opportunity training" throughout the week.

- Visualization techniques can be performed before, during or after physical training.

- Meditation sessions can be conducted before or after physical training.

- Controlled breathing exercises can be conducted before, during or after physical training.

- Don't be apprehensive to change things around. Remember, nothing is set in stone.

- Encourage friendly and healthy competition between your training partner.

- Always maintain a professional attitude when training.

- Don't expect to be perfect when training.

- Don't let incorrect habits go uncorrected.

- Don't get frustrated. Remember, it's a learning process that takes time.

- Make full use of your rest days. Remember, resting the body is just as important as training. Training intensely day after day will lead to either burnout or injury. The body needs time to recoup and replenish itself from grueling workouts. Remember, there is growth in rest.

- Since physical fitness goals will vary from person to person, you'll need to incorporate your current fitness/workout regimen (i.e., weight training, CrossFit, cardio training, etc.) into your mental toughness program. How you do this, is entirely up to you.

Finding the Right Training Partner

As I discussed earlier, many of these mental toughness exercises can be performed individually, while others will require the assistance of a training partner, instructor or coach.

A good training partner should motivate, challenge and push you to your limits. He or she doesn't have to share the same goals as you do, but they must be willing to help you reach your full potential. Your training partner or coach should also be somewhat familiar with the various combat drills and equipment. For example, they should know how to hold and manipulate the focus mitts, perform training simulations, and perform full-contact exercises.

While a good training partner can be a major asset, having a bad one can be a major liability. Be exceptionally careful who you choose to train with you. When looking for a training parter, try to avoid the following personality types:

1. **The conversationalist** - someone who talks too much and often disrupts the training intensity.

2. **The challenger** - someone who is naturally argumentative and tries to test your knowledge and patience.

3. **The ego tripper** - someone who will do anything to prove just how tough he is. He usually enjoys full-contact drills and

likes to injure others in training.

4. **The insecure one** - someone who is hesitant to participate in training full-contact drills and exercises.

5. **The know-it-all** - someone who thinks he knows anything and everything about mental toughness training.

6. **The dilettante** - someone who doesn't understand the importance of mental toughness training, and therefore doesn't fully commit himself to the program.

Finally, remember that a good training partner or coach is there to evaluate your performance during your workouts. Listen carefully to what he has to say. A good coach, for example, will be brutally honest and tell you what you are doing correctly and what you are doing wrong. Learn to put your ego aside and heed his advice.

Safety When Training

Safety precautions must always be taken when engaged in mental toughness training. Remember, a serious injury can set you back for weeks and even months. Don't make the mistake of letting your ego or laziness get the best of you. Learn to be safety-conscious. Here are a few suggestions to help minimize the possibilities of injury when training:

1. Buy the best training equipment that you can afford.

2. Know the proper way to use training equipment.

3. Regularly inspect your equipment for wear and defects.

4. Avoid ego-driven training partners or coaches.

5. Be especially aware when training with someone of superior size, skill, or experience.

6. Always warm up before training.

7. Drink plenty of water during training sessions to avoid dehydration.

8. Be cautious when performing training drills for the first time.

It's also a good idea to have a first-aid kit nearby. A first-aid kit is intended for both minor and major injuries. The kit should be kept in a well-sealed box away from children. Don't forget to write down the emergency number for your local hospital or medical clinic on the box. Most first-aid kits can be purchased at your local drugstore. Each kit should contain cotton wool and hydrogen peroxide for cleaning cuts, tweezers, scissors, triangular bandages, alcohol swabs, adhesive tape, adhesive bandages, antibiotic ointment, sterile pads, gauze bandages, and elastic bandages for sprains and for elbow and knee injuries.

Avoiding Overtraining & Burnout

Burnout is defined as a negative emotional state acquired by physical overtraining. Some symptoms of burnout include physical illness, boredom, anxiety, disinterest in training, and general sluggish behavior. Whether you are a beginner or expert, you're susceptible to burnout. Here are a few suggestions to help avoid burnout in your training:

1. Make your workouts intense but enjoyable.

2. Vary your training routine (i.e., hard day/easy day routine).

3. Train to different types of music.

4. Pace yourself during your workouts - don't try to do it all in one day.

5. Listen to your body- if you don't feel up to training, skip a day.

6. Work out in different types of environments.

7. Use different types of training equipment.

8. Workout with different training partners.

9. Keep accurate records of your training routine.

10. Vary the intensity of your training throughout your workout.

Keeping Track of Your Training

In order to reap the full benefits of training, you need to keep track of your workouts and monitor your progress. Monitoring your training will give you a wide range of benefits, including:

1. Help determine if you making progress in your training.

2. The ability to effectively alter your training program.

3. Track your rate of progress,

4. Stay interested and motivated.

5. Break through performance plateaus.

Two of the best tools for keeping track of your training progress are: the training journal and video footage. Let's take a look at each one.

The Training Journal

Record keeping is one of the most important and often neglected aspects of mental toughness training. Try to make it a habit to keep accurate records of your workouts in a personal journal. This type of record keeping is important for some of the following reasons:

1. It will help you monitor your progress.

2. It will keep you organized.

3. It will inspire, motivate and remind you to stick to your goals.

4. It helps prevent potential injuries.

5. It will help you guard against over training.

6. If you are learning new skills, it accelerates the learning process.

7. It gives you valuable training information that can be analyzed.

8. It helps you determine which drills, activities, and exercises are unproductive.

9. It helps you determine which activities are helpful and productive.

10. When making entries into your journal, don't forget to include some of the following important details:

11. The date and time you trained.

12. The mental toughness skill or attribute you are training.

13. The types of drills and exercises you performed.

14. The number or sets, reps you performed for each exercise or drill.

15. The number or rounds and minutes per round you performed for each drill or exercise.

16. The mental toughness skill or attribute you worked on.

17. The feelings you experienced before, during, and after your workout.

18. Your overall mood.

19. Concerns you have about your current training.

20. Comments, ideas and observations made by your coach, training partner or instructor.

Videotaping

If you really want to actually see your progress, videotape your workouts. The video will provide you with a more accurate picture of what you are doing in your training. You will be able to observe mistakes and recognize your strengths and weaknesses. The video footage will also motivate you to train harder. Remember to date each videotape or video clip; later on you will be able to compare and see marked improvements in your training performance.

Chapter Eight
Inspiring Words to Live By

Treasured Words

Here is a compilation of inspiring and motivational quotes culled from around the world and throughout history. They speak the time-tested truth of real human competition and confrontation. Moreover, they both inspire and instruct and will no doubt be used and re-used by those who have heard them. I modestly hope that they will also lead you through the trials and tribulations of your own struggles and incumbent triumphs.

"A person who never made a mistake never tried anything new."

-Albert Einstein

"Do not dwell in the past, do not dream of the future, concentrate the mind on the present moment."

-Buddha

"The secret of happiness is freedom. The secret of freedom is courage."

-Thucydides

"The harder you work, the harder it is to surrender."

-Vince Lombardi

"Build up your weaknesses until they become your strong points."

-Knute Rockne

"Victory belongs to the most persevering."

      -Napoleon

"However difficult life may seem, there is always something you can do and succeed at."

      -Stephen Hawking

"To change ones life, start immediately, do it flamboyantly, no exceptions."

      -William James

"Fortune favours the bold."

      -Virgil

"Winners make goals, losers make excuses."

      -Author Unknown

"Self-control is the chief element in self-respect, and self-respect is the chief element in courage."

      -Thucydides

"We are what we repeatedly do. Excellence, therefore, is not an act but a habit."

      -Aristotle

Invincible

"Every strike brings me closer to the next home run."

-Babe Ruth

"It does not matter how slowly you go as long as you do not stop."

-Confucius

"Our greatest weakness lies in giving up. The most certain way to succeed is always to try just one more time."

-Thomas A. Edison

"If you always put limit on everything you do, physical or anything else. It will spread into your work and into your life. There are no limits. There are only plateaus, and you must not stay there, you must go beyond them."

-Bruce Lee

"Genius is one percent inspiration and ninety-nine percent perspiration."

-Thomas Edison

"You have to learn the rules of the game. And then you have to play better than anyone else."

-Albert Einstein

"The secret of getting ahead is getting started."

-Mark Twain

"Quality is not an act, it is a habit."

　　　　　　-Aristotle

"What you get by achieving your goals is not as important as what you become by achieving your goals."

　　　　　　-Henry David Thoreau

"He who knows himself is enlightened."

　　　　　　-Lao Tzu

"Well done is better than well said."

　　　　　　-Benjamin Franklin

"The spirit, the will to win, and the will to excel, are the things that endure. These qualities are so much more important than the events that occur."

　　　　　　-Vincent Lombardi

"The key to immortality is first living a life worth remembering."

　　　　　　-Bruce Lee

"Pursue one great decisive aim with force and determination."

　　　　　　-Carl von Clausewitz

Invincible

"Every calamity is to be overcome by endurance."

-Virgil

"There's a way to do it better - find it."

-Thomas A. Edison

"Motivation is the art of getting people to do what you want them to do because they want to do it."

-Dwight D. Eisenhower

"No one saves us but ourselves. No one can and no one may. We ourselves must walk the path."

-Buddha

"There is only one way to happiness and that is to cease worrying about things which are beyond the power of our will."

-Epictetus

"Show me a good and gracious loser and I'll show you a failure."

-Knute Rockne

"A man's worth is no greater than the worth of his ambitions."

-Marcus Aurelius

"Know or listen to those who know."

-Baltasar Gracian

"Self trust is the essence of heroism."

-Emerson

"Intelligence is the ability to adapt to change."

-Stephen Hawking

"Weakness of attitude becomes weakness of character."

-Albert Einstein

"At the center of your being you have the answer; you know who you are and you know what you want."

-Lao Tzu

"My friend...care for your psyche...know thyself, for once we know ourselves, we may learn how to care for ourselves"

-Socrates

"Your visions will become clear only when you can look into your own heart. Who looks outside, dreams; who looks inside, awakes."

-C.G. Jung

"Adversity is the first path to truth."

        -Lord Byron

"The key to growth is the introduction of higher dimensions of consciousness into our awareness."

        -Lao Tzu

"It had long since come to my attention that people of accomplishment rarely sat back and let things happen to them. They went out and happened to things."

        -Leonardo da Vinci

"Perfection is achieved, not when there is nothing more to add, but when there is nothing left to take away."

        -Antoine de Saint-Exupéry

"To hell with circumstances; I create opportunities."

        -Bruce Lee

"The only safety for the conquered is to expect no safety."

        -Virgil

"The mind is everything. What you think you become."

        -Buddha

Chapter Eight: Inspiring Words to Live By

"To be a man is, precisely, to be responsible."

-Antoine de Saint-Exupéry

"You will never do anything in this world without courage. It is the greatest quality of the mind next to honor."

-Aristotle

"Victory belongs to the most persevering."

-Napoleon Bonaparte

"Courage is grace under pressure."

-Ernest Hemingway

"The most vital quality a soldier can possess is self-confidence, utter, complete and bumptious."

-General Patton

"I wouldn't give a tinker's damn for a man who isn't sometimes afraid. Fear's the spice that makes it interesting to go ahead."

-Daniel Boone

"The difference between a successful person and others is not a lack of strength, not a lack of knowledge, but rather in a lack of will."

-Vince Lombard

Invincible

"*What measures will ensure the soldiers will be victorious? Control is foremost.*"

-Wu Qi

"*Adversity has the effect of eliciting talents, which in prosperous circumstances would have lain dormant.*"

-Horace

"*Courage is what it takes to stand up and speak; courage is also what it takes to sit down and listen.*"

-Winston Churchill

"*I count him braver who overcomes his desires than him who conquers his enemies; for the hardest victory is over self.*"

-Aristotle

"*A superior man is modest in his speech, but exceeds in his actions.*"

-Confucius

"*Brave men rejoice in adversity, just as brave soldiers triumph in war.*"

-Lucius Annaeus Seneca

"*I have with me two gods, Persuasion and Compulsion.*"

-Themistocles

Chapter Eight: Inspiring Words to Live By

"We have nothing left in the world but what we can win with our swords. Timidity and cowardice are for men who can see safety at their backs - who can retreat without molestation along some easy road and find refuge in the familiar fields of their native land; but they are not for you: you must be brave; for you there is no middle way between victory or death - put all hope of it from you, and either conquer, or, should fortune hesitate to favour you, meet death in battle rather than in flight."

-Hannibal

"If one does not know to which port is sailing, no wind is favorable."

-Lucius Annaeus Seneca

"The possession of anything begins in the mind."

-Bruce Lee

"If you're afraid of anything, why not take a chance and do the thing you fear? Sometimes it's the only way to get over being afraid."

-Audie Murphy

"This above all; to thine own self be true."

-William Shakespeare

Invincible

"In battle it is the cowards who run the most risk; bravery is a rampart of defense."

-Sallust

"Courage is rightly esteemed the first of human qualities, because... it is the quality that guarantees all others."

-Winston Churchill

"When it is obvious that the goals cannot be reached, don't adjust the goals, adjust the action steps."

-Confucius

"No man is free who is not master of himself."

-Epictetus

"And above all you ought to guard against leading an army to fight which is afraid or which is not confident of victory. For the greatest sign of an impending loss is when one does not believe one can win."

-Machiavelli

"It seems to be a law of nature, inflexible and inexorable, that those who will not risk cannot win."

-Admiral John Paul Jones

"History does not long entrust the care of freedom to the weak or the timid." -Dwight D. Eisenhower

"Though an army should encamp against me, my heart shall not fear; though war should rise against me, in this I will be confident."

-King David

"It is better to conquer yourself than to win a thousand battles. Then the victory is yours. It cannot be taken from you, not by angels or by demons, heaven or hell."

-Buddha

"If we did the things we are capable of, we would astound ourselves."

-Thomas Edison

"Soldiers must be treated in the first instance with humanity, but kept under control by means of iron discipline. This is a certain road to victory."

-Sun Tzu

"The longer we dwell on our misfortunes, the greater is their power to harm us."

-Voltaire

"He who fears being conquered is sure of defeat."

-Napoleon Bonaparte

Invincible

"It is not only for what we do that we are held responsible, but also for what we do not do."

-Moliere

"It is better to offer no excuse than a bad one."

-George Washington

"Let me embrace thee, sour adversity, for wise men say it is the wisest course."

-William Shakespeare

"Untutored courage is useless in the face of educated bullets."

-General Patton

"It often requires more courage to dare to do right than to fear to do wrong."

-Abraham Lincoln

"The strong do what they have to do and the weak accept what they have to accept."

-Thucydides

"Time stays long enough for anyone who will use it."

-Leonardo da Vinci

"I am not afraid of an army of lions led by a sheep; I am afraid of an army of sheep led by a lion."

-Alexander the Great

"When soldiers have been baptized in the fire of a battlefield, they have all one rank in my eyes."

-Napoleon Bonaparte

"So it is with the Spartans; fighting singly, they are as good as any, but fighting together, they are the best soldiers in the world."

-Demaratus

"Happiness lies in the joy of achievement and the thrill of creative effort."

-Franklin D. Roosevelt

"Discipline is the soul of an army. It makes small numbers formidable; procures success to the weak, and esteem to all."

-George Washington

"In war discipline is superior to strength."

-Vegetius

"You're never beaten until you admit it."

-General Patton

Invincible

"It's not that I'm so smart, it's just that I stay with problems longer."

-Albert Einstein

"But it might be closer to the truth to assume that the faculty known as self-control - the gift of keeping calm even under the greatest stress - is rooted in temperament. It is itself an emotion which serves to balance the passionate feelings in strong characters without destroying them, and it is this balance alone that assures the dominance of the intellect..."

-Karl von Clausewitz

"You don't develop courage by being happy in your relationships everyday. You develop it by surviving difficult times and challenging adversity."

-Epicurus

"Impossible is a word to be found only in the dictionary of fools."

-Napoleon Bonaparte

"Fury itself supplies arms."

-Virgil

"The price of greatness is responsibility."

-Winston Churchill

Chapter Eight: Inspiring Words to Live By

"To be idle is a short road to death and to be diligent is a way of life; foolish people are idle, wise people are diligent."

-*Buddha*

"The will to win, the desire to succeed, the urge to reach your full potential... these are the keys that will unlock the door to personal excellence."

-*Confucius*

"I have the simplest tastes. I am always satisfied with the best."

-*Oscar Wilde*

"Veni, Vidi, Vici." (I came, I saw, I conquered.)

-*Julius Caesar*

"Who dares wins."

-*Motto of the Special Air Services (SAS)*

"Every man dies. Not every man really lives."

-*William Wallace*

"There is nothing impossible to him who will try."

-*Alexander the Great*

Invincible

"Don't leave a stone unturned. It's always something, to know you have done the most you could."

-Charles Dickens

"A good decision is based on knowledge and not on numbers."

-Plato

"To be happy is to be able to become aware of oneself without fright."

-Walter Benjamin

"No man ever reached to excellence in any one art or profession without having passed through the slow and painful process of study and preparation."

-Horace

"When you were riding on the crest of a wave, you were most likely to be missing out on something."

-Knute Rockne

"The first requisite for success is the ability to apply your physical and mental energies to one problem incessantly without growing weary."

-Thomas Edison

Final Words

There are many tough people out there. In fact, they reside in every city in every country. However, most are nothing more than aggressive brutes who lack self-mastery. And self-mastery is what separates the superior human being from all others.

There is a spiritual aspect to mental toughness. However, I am not referring to religious dogma or beliefs when I speak of a spiritual component. In fact, the spiritual aspects of mental toughness are not something that is taught or studied. Rather, it is that which transcends the physical and intellectual aspects of being and reality. Ancient mystics referred to it as that which cannot be named. Whether you name it or not, it's real. There is a deeper part of each of us that is a tremendous source of truth and achievement.

The paths to self-enlightenment are many, but the destination is singular. During the challenging quest of mental toughness training, one begins to tap the higher qualities of human nature - those elements of our being that inherently enable us to know right from wrong and good from evil. As we slowly develop this aspect of our total self, we begin to strengthen qualities profoundly important to the "way." Such qualities are essential to your growth through the mastery of inner peace, the clarity of your vision, and your realization of universal truths.

Invincible

The spiritual component of mental toughness is truly the most difficult aspect of personal growth. Unlike the physical elements, where the practitioner's abilities will be restricted to some degree by genetics and other natural factors, the spiritual component offers unlimited potential for personal growth and development. In the final analysis, the spiritual aspect of mental toughness poses the greatest challenges and the greatest rewards. It truly is an open-ended plane of unlimited advancement.

I wish you the best of luck in your journey!

-Sammy Franco

Appendix

Combat Skills

In this section, I am going to teach you the foundational combat skills required to perform all of the mental toughness drills featured in this book. These basic skills include the fighting stance, mobility and footwork, punching, kicking, blocking, and parrying techniques. Let's begin with the fighting stance.

The Fighting Stance

The fighting stance defines your ability to execute both offensive and defensive techniques, and it will play a material role in the outcome of a combat situation. It stresses strategic soundness and simplicity over complexity and style. The fighting stance also facilitates optimum execution of your body weapons while simultaneously protecting your vital targets against quick counter strikes.

The fighting stance is designed around the centerline. The centerline is an imaginary vertical line running through the center of the body, from the top of your head to the bottom of the groin. Most of your vital targets are situated along this line, including the head, throat, solar plexus, and groin. Obviously, you want to avoid directly exposing your centerline to the assailant. To achieve this, position your feet and body at a 45-degree angle

Pictured here, a right lead fighting stance.

from the opponent. This moves your body targets back and away from direct strikes but leaves you strategically positioned to attack.

When assuming a fighting stance, place your strongest and most coordinated side forward. For example, a right-handed person stands with his or her right side toward the assailant. Keeping your strongest side forward enhances the speed, power, and accuracy of your strike. This doesn't mean that you should never practice fighting from your other side. You must be capable of fighting from both sides, and you should spend equal practice time on the left and right stances.

Many people make the costly mistake of stepping forward to assume a fighting stance. Do not do this! This action only moves you closer to your assailant before your protective structure is soundly established. Moving closer to your assailant also dramatically reduces your defensive reaction time. So get into the habit of stepping backward to assume your stance. Practice this daily until it becomes a natural and economical movement.

How to Assume a Fighting Stance

When assuming your fighting stance, place your feet about shoulder width apart. Keep your knees bent and flexible. Think of your legs as power springs to launch you through the ranges of unarmed combat (kicking, punching, and grappling range).

Mobility is also important, as we'll discuss later. All footwork and strategic movement should be performed on the balls of your feet. Your weight distribution is also an important factor. Since combat is dynamic, your weight distribution will frequently change. However, when stationary, keep 50 percent of your body weight on each leg and always be in control of it.

The hands are aligned one behind the other along your centerline. The lead arm is held high and bent at approximately 90 degrees. The rear arm is kept back by the chin. Arranged this way, the hands not only protect the upper centerline but also allow quick deployment of your body weapons. When holding your guard, do not tighten your shoulder or arm muscles prior to striking. Stay relaxed and loose. Finally, keep your chin slightly angled down. This diminishes target size and reduces the likelihood of a paralyzing blow to your chin or a lethal strike to your throat.

The best method for practicing your fighting stance is in front of a full-length mirror. Place the mirror in an area that allows sufficient room for movement; a garage or basement is perfect. Stand in front of the mirror, far enough away to see your entire body. Stand naturally with your arms relaxed at your sides. Now close your eyes and quickly assume your fighting stance. Open your eyes and check for flaws. Look for low hand guards, improper foot positioning or body angle, rigid shoulders and knees, etc. Drill this way repeatedly, working from both the right and left side. Practice this until your fighting stance becomes second nature.

Footwork & Mobility

Next are footwork and mobility. I define mobility as the ability to move your body quickly and freely, which is accomplished through basic footwork. The safest footwork involves quick, economical steps performed on the balls of your feet, while you remain relaxed and balanced. Keep in mind that balance is your most important consideration.

Basic footwork can be used for both offensive and defensive purposes, and it is structured around four general directions: forward, backward, right, and left. However, always remember this footwork rule of thumb: Always move the foot closest to the direction you want to go first, and let the other foot follow an equal distance. This prevents cross-stepping, which can cost you your life in a high-risk combat situation.

Basic Footwork Movements

1. Moving forward (advance)- from your fighting stance, first move your front foot forward (approximately 12 inches) and then move your rear foot an equal distance.

2. Moving backward (retreat) - from your fighting stance, first move your rear foot backward (approximately 12 inches) and then move your front foot an equal distance.

3. Moving right (sidestep right) - from your fighting stance, first move your right foot to the right (approximately 12 inches) and then move your left foot an equal distance.

4. Moving left (sidestep left) - from your fighting stance, first move your left foot to the left (approximately 12 inches) and then move your right foot an equal distance.

Practice these four movements for 10 to 15 minutes a day in front of a full-length mirror. In a couple weeks, your footwork should be quick, balanced, and natural.

Circling Right and Left

Strategic circling is an advanced form of footwork where you will use your front leg as a pivot point. This type of movement can also be used defensively to evade an overwhelming assault or to strike the opponent from various strategic angles. Strategic circling can be performed from either a left or right stance.

Circling left (from a left stance) - this means you'll be moving your body around the opponent in a clockwise direction. From a left stance, step 8 to 12 inches to the left with your left foot, then use your left leg as a pivot point and wheel your entire rear leg to the left until the correct stance and positioning is acquired.

Circling right (from a right stance) - from a right stance, step 8 to 12 inches to the right with your right foot, then use your right leg as a pivot point and wheel your entire rear leg to the right until the correct stance and positioning is acquired.

Kicking Techniques

While there are a myriad of kicking techniques in the martial arts world, we are only going to focus on five basic skills. They are:

- **Push kick (from the front and back legs)**
- **Side kick (from the front leg)**
- **Hook kick (from the front and back legs)**

Push Kick (front leg)

1. To perform the kick, begin from a fighting stance.

2. While maintaining your balance, shift your weight onto your back leg and raise your front leg up (your front knee should be bent at approximately 90 degrees).

3. Next, thrust with your hips and drive the ball of your front foot into the target.

4. After contact is made with the target, quickly retract your leg to the starting position. Remember to always keep your hands up when performing kicking techniques.

When performing the push kick be certain to make contact with the ball of your foot and not your toes. Striking the opponent with your toes can easily lead to a severe injury.

Push Kick (back leg)

1. To perform the kick, begin from a fighting stance.

2. While maintaining your balance, push your back foot off the ground and shift your weight to your front leg (your rear

knee should be bent at approximately 90 degrees).

3. Next, thrust with your hips and drive the ball of your foot into the target.

4. After contact is made with the target, quickly retract your leg to the starting position. Again, make certain to make contact with the ball of your foot and not your toes.

Pictured here, a push kick delivered from the front leg.

Side Kick (front leg)

1. To perform the kick, begin from a fighting stance.

2. While maintaining your balance, lean back and shift your weight onto your rear leg while simultaneously pivoting your body so your centerline is approximately 90 degrees from the opponent.

3. Raise your front knee up and close to your body (this is called the "chamber" position).

4. Next, use your hips and thrust your front leg forcefully into

the target. Contact is made with the heel of your foot.

5. After contact is made with the target, retract your leg to the starting position.

Pictured here, a side kick.

Hook Kick (front leg)

1. To perform the kick, begin from a fighting stance.

2. While maintaining your balance, lean back slightly and shift your weight to your rear leg.

3. Simultaneously raise your front knee up and towards the opponent.

4. Next, quickly twist your front hip and swing your lead leg forcefully into the opponent. Your front knee should be slightly bent when impact is made with the target. Avoid snapping your knee when performing the kick. Contact should be made with either the dorsum of your foot or shin bone.

5. After contact is made with the opponent, bring your leg back to the starting position.

Hook Kick (back leg)

1. To perform the kick, begin from a fighting stance.

2. While maintaining your balance, push off the back foot and shift your weight forward.

3. Next, raise your rear knee up and twist your hips forward as you swing your rear leg forcefully into the opponent.

4. Your rear knee should be slightly bent when impact is made with the target. Avoid snapping your knee when performing the hook kick. Once again, contact should be made with either the dorsum of your foot or shin bone.

5. After contact is made with the target, bring your leg back to the starting position.

The hook kick.

Punching Techniques

In this section, I'm going to teach you four different punching skills that can be used in some of the mental toughness exercises. They are:

- **Lead straight**
- **Rear cross**
- **Hook punch**
- **Uppercut punch**

The Lead Straight Punch

The lead straight is a linear punch thrown from your lead arm, and contact is made with the center knuckle. To execute the technique, perform the following steps.

1. Start off in a fighting stance with both of your hands held up in the guard position. Your fists should be lightly clenched with both of your elbows pointing to the ground.

2. Simultaneously step toward the opponent and twist your front waist and shoulder forward as you snap your front arm into the target.

3. When delivering the punch, remember not to lock out your arm as this will have a "pushing effect" on the target.

4. Quickly retract your arm back to the starting position.

5. One common mistake when throwing the punch is to let it deflect off to the side of the target. Also, keep in mind that lead straight punches can be delivered to the opponent's head or body. Targets for the lead straight include the opponent's nose, chin, and solar plexus.

Pictured here, a lead straight punch.

Rear Cross

The rear cross is considered the heavy artillery of punches and it's thrown from your rear arm. To execute the punch, perform the following steps:

1. Start off in a fighting stance with both of your hands held up in the guard position. Your fists should be lightly clenched with both of your elbows pointing to the ground.

2. Next, quickly twist your rear hips and shoulders forward as you snap your rear arm into the target. Proper waist twisting and weight transfer is of paramount importance to the rear cross. You must shift your weight from your rear foot to your lead leg as you throw the punch.

3. To maximize the impact of the punch, make certain that your fist is positioned horizontally. Avoid overextending the blow or exposing your chin during its execution.

4. Once again, do not lock out your arm when throwing the

punch. Let the power of the blow sink into the target before you retract it back to the starting position.

The rear cross.

Hook Punch

The hook is another devastating punch in your arsenal, yet it's also one of the most difficult to master. This punch can be performed from either your front or rear hand, and it can be delivered to both high or low targets.

1. Start in a fighting stance with your hand guard held up. Both of your elbows should be pointing to the ground, and your fists clenched loosely.

2. Next, quickly and smoothly, raise your elbow up so that your arm is parallel to the ground while simultaneously torquing your shoulder, hip, and foot into the direction of the blow.

3. When delivering the strike, be certain your arm is bent at least ninety degrees and that your wrist and forearm are kept

straight throughout the movement.

4. As you throw the punch, your fist is positioned vertically. The elbow should be locked when contact is made with the target. Remember to simultaneously tighten your fists when impact is made with the target. This action will allow your punch to travel with optimum speed and efficiency, and it will also augment the impact power of your strike.

5. Return to the starting position.

The lead hook punch.

Uppercut Punch

The uppercut is a another powerful punch that can be delivered from both the lead and rear arm. To execute the blow, perform the following steps.

1. Start off in a fighting stance with both of your hands held up in the guard position. Your fists should be lightly clenched with both of your elbows pointing to the ground.

2. Next, drop your shoulder and bend your knees.

3. Quickly, stand up and drive your fist upward and into the target. Your palm should be facing you when contact is made with the target. To avoid any possible injury, always keep your wrists straight.

4. Make certain your punch has a tight arc. Avoid "winding up" the blow. A properly executed uppercut punch should be a tight explosive jolt.

5. Return to the fighting stance.

The lead uppercut punch.

The rear uppercut.

Blocking Techniques

Blocks are defensive techniques designed to intercept your assailant's circular attacks. They are performed by placing a non-vital body part between the opponent's strike and your anatomical body target. There are three primary blocks you need to learn. They are:

- **high block**
- **mid block**
- **elbow block**

High Block

The high block is used to defend against overhead blows. To execute the lead high block, simply raise your lead arm up and extend your forearm out and above your head. Make certain that your hand is open and not clenched. This will increase the surface area of your block and provide a quick counterattack. The mechanics for the lead high block are the same as for the rear high block. Raise your rear arm up and extend your forearm out and above your head.

The high block.

Mid Block

The mid-block is specifically used to defend against circular blows to your head or upper torso. To perform the move, raise either your right or left arm at approximately 90 degrees while simultaneously pronating (rotating) it into the direction of the strike. Make contact with the belly of your forearm at the assailant's wrist or forearm. This movement will provide maximum structural integrity for the blocking tool. Make certain that your hand is held open to increase the surface area of your block. When performing the mid-block, be certain to time the rotation of your arm with the attack. Don't forget that the mid-block has both height (up and down) and width (in and out) fluctuations that are relative to the characteristics of the assailant's blow.

The lead hand mid block.

In this photo, a rear hand mid block.

Elbow Block

The elbow block is used to stop circular blows to your midsection, such as uppercuts, shovel hooks, and hook kicks. To execute the move, drop your elbow and simultaneously twist your body toward your centerline. Be certain to keep your elbow perpendicular to the floor with your hands relaxed and close to your chest. The elbow block can be used on both the right and left sides.

Pictured here, the elbow block.

Parrying Techniques

The parry is a quick, forceful slap that redirects your assailant's linear strike (jabs, lead straights, and rear crosses). There are two general types of parries, horizontal and vertical, and both can be performed with the right and left hands.

Horizontal Parry

To properly execute a horizontal parry from a fighting stance, move your lead hand horizontally across your body to deflect and redirect the assailant's punch. Immediately return to your guard position. Be certain to make contact with the palm of your hand.

Pictured here, a right hand horizontal parry.

Vertical Parry

To execute a vertical parry, from a fighting stance, move your hand vertically down your body to deflect and redirect the assailant's blow. Once again, don't forget to counterattack your opponent. A word of caution, don't parry punches with your finger. The fingers provide no structural integrity, and they can be jammed or broken easily.

Invincible

Glossary

A

accuracy—The precise or exact projection of force. Accuracy is also defined as the ability to execute a combative movement with precision and exactness.

adaptability—The ability to physically and psychologically adjust to new or different conditions or circumstances of combat.

advanced first-strike tools—Offensive techniques that are specifically used when confronted with multiple opponents.

aerobic exercise—Literally, "with air." Exercise that elevates the heart rate to a training level for a prolonged period of time, usually 30 minutes.

affective preparedness – One of the three components of preparedness. Affective preparedness means being emotionally, philosophically, and spiritually prepared for the strains of combat. See cognitive preparedness and psychomotor preparedness.

aggression—Hostile and injurious behavior directed toward a person.

aggressive response—One of the three possible counters when assaulted by a grab, choke, or hold from a standing position. Aggressive response requires you to counter the enemy with destructive blows and strikes. See moderate response and passive response.

aggressive hand positioning—Placement of hands so as to imply aggressive or hostile intentions.

agility—An attribute of combat. One's ability to move his or her body quickly and gracefully.

amalgamation—A scientific process of uniting or merging.

ambidextrous—The ability to perform with equal facility on both the right and left sides of the body.

anabolic steroids – synthetic chemical compounds that resemble the male sex hormone testosterone. This performance-enhancing drug is known to increase lean muscle mass, strength, and endurance.

analysis and integration—One of the five elements of CFA's mental component. This is the painstaking process of breaking down various elements, concepts, sciences, and disciplines into their atomic parts, and then methodically and strategically analyzing, experimenting, and drastically modifying the information so that it fulfills three combative requirements: efficiency, effectiveness, and safety. Only then is it finally integrated into the CFA system.

anatomical striking targets—The various anatomical body targets that can be struck and which are especially vulnerable to potential harm. They include: the eyes, temple, nose, chin, back of neck, front of neck, solar plexus, ribs, groin, thighs, knees, shins, and instep.

anchoring – The strategic process of trapping the assailant's neck or limb in order to control the range of engagement during razing.

assailant—A person who threatens or attacks another person.

assault—The threat or willful attempt to inflict injury upon the person of another.

assault and battery—The unlawful touching of another person without justification.

assessment—The process of rapidly gathering, analyzing, and accurately evaluating information in terms of threat and danger. You can assess people, places, actions, and objects.

attack—Offensive action designed to physically control, injure, or kill another person.

attitude—One of the three factors that determine who wins a street fight. Attitude means being emotionally, philosophically, and spiritually liberated from societal and religious mores. See skills and knowledge.

attributes of combat—The physical, mental, and spiritual qualities that enhance combat skills and tactics.

awareness—Perception or knowledge of people, places, actions, and objects. (In CFA, there are three categories of tactical awareness: criminal awareness, situational awareness, and self-awareness.)

B

balance—One's ability to maintain equilibrium while stationary or moving.

blading the body—Strategically positioning your body at a 45-degree angle.

blitz and disengage—A style of sparring whereby a fighter moves into a range of combat, unleashes a strategic compound attack, and then quickly disengages to a safe distance. Of all sparring methodologies, the blitz and disengage most closely resembles a real street fight.

block—A defensive tool designed to intercept the assailant's attack by placing a non-vital target between the assailant's strike and your vital body target.

body composition—The ratio of fat to lean body tissue.

body language—Nonverbal communication through posture, gestures, and facial expressions.

body mechanics—Technically precise body movement during the execution of a body weapon, defensive technique, or other fighting maneuver.

body tackle – A tackle that occurs when your opponent haphazardly rushes forward and plows his body into yours.

body weapon—Also known as a tool, one of the various body parts that can be used to strike or otherwise injure or kill a criminal assailant.

burn out—A negative emotional state acquired by physically over- training. Some symptoms include: illness, boredom, anxiety, disinterest in training, and general sluggishness.

C

cadence—Coordinating tempo and rhythm to establish a timing pattern of movement.

cardiorespiratory conditioning—The component of physical fitness that deals with the heart, lungs, and circulatory system.

centerline—An imaginary vertical line that divides your body in half and which contains many of your vital anatomical targets.

choke holds—Holds that impair the flow of blood or oxygen to the brain.

circular movements—Movements that follow the direction of a curve.

close-quarter combat—One of the three ranges of knife and bludgeon combat. At this distance, you can strike, slash, or stab your assailant with a variety of close-quarter techniques.

cognitive development—One of the five elements of CFA's mental component. The process of developing and enhancing your fighting skills through specific mental exercises and techniques. See analysis and integration, killer instinct, philosophy, and strategic/tactical development.

cognitive exercises—Various mental exercises used to enhance fighting skills and tactics.

cognitive preparedness – One of the three components of preparedness. Cognitive preparedness means being equipped with the strategic concepts, principles, and general knowledge of combat. See affective preparedness and psychomotor preparedness.

combat-oriented training—Training that is specifically related to the harsh realities of both armed and unarmed combat. See ritual-oriented training and sport-oriented training.

combative arts—The various arts of war. See martial arts.

combative attributes—See attributes of combat.

combative fitness—A state characterized by cardiorespiratory and muscular/skeletal conditioning, as well as proper body composition.

combative mentality—Also known as the killer instinct, this is a combative state of mind necessary for fighting. See killer instinct.

combat ranges—The various ranges of unarmed combat.

combative utility—The quality of condition of being combatively useful.

combination(s)—See compound attack.

common peroneal nerve—A pressure point area located approximately four to six inches above the knee on the midline of the outside of the thigh.

composure—A combative attribute. Composure is a quiet and focused mind-set that enables you to acquire your combative agenda.

compound attack—One of the five conventional methods of attack. Two or more body weapons launched in strategic succession whereby the fighter overwhelms his assailant with a flurry of full speed, full-force blows.

conditioning training—A CFA training methodology requiring the practitioner to deliver a variety of offensive and defensive combinations for a 4-minute period. See proficiency training and street training.

contact evasion—Physically moving or manipulating your body to avoid being tackled by the adversary.

Contemporary Fighting Arts—A modern martial art and self-defense system made up of three parts: physical, mental, and spiritual.

conventional ground-fighting tools—Specific ground-fighting techniques designed to control, restrain, and temporarily incapacitate your adversary. Some conventional ground fighting tactics include: submission holds, locks, certain choking techniques, and specific striking techniques.

coordination—A physical attribute characterized by the ability to perform a technique or movement with efficiency, balance, and accuracy.

counterattack—Offensive action made to counter an assailant's initial attack.

courage—A combative attribute. The state of mind and spirit that enables a fighter to face danger and vicissitudes with confidence, resolution, and bravery.

creatine monohydrate—A tasteless and odorless white powder that mimics some of the effects of anabolic steroids. Creatine is a safe body-building product that can benefit anyone who wants to increase their strength, endurance, and lean muscle mass.

criminal awareness—One of the three categories of CFA awareness. It involves a general understanding and knowledge of the nature and dynamics of a criminal's motivations, mentalities, methods, and capabilities to perpetrate violent crime. See situational awareness and self-awareness.

criminal justice—The study of criminal law and the procedures associated with its enforcement.

criminology—The scientific study of crime and criminals.

cross-stepping—The process of crossing one foot in front of or behind the other when moving.

crushing tactics—Nuclear grappling-range techniques designed to crush the assailant's anatomical targets.

cue word - a unique word or personal statement that helps focus your attention on the execution of a skill, instead of its outcome.

D

deadly force—Weapons or techniques that may result in unconsciousness, permanent disfigurement, or death.

deception—A combative attribute. A stratagem whereby you delude your assailant.

decisiveness—A combative attribute. The ability to follow a tactical course of action that is unwavering and focused.

defense—The ability to strategically thwart an assailant's attack (armed or unarmed).

defensive flow—A progression of continuous defensive responses.

defensive mentality—A defensive mind-set.

defensive reaction time—The elapsed time between an assailant's physical attack and your defensive response to that attack. See offensive reaction time.

demeanor—A person's outward behavior. One of the essential factors to consider when assessing a threatening individual.

diet—A lifestyle of healthy eating.

disingenuous vocalization—The strategic and deceptive

utilization of words to successfully launch a preemptive strike at your adversary.

distancing—The ability to quickly understand spatial relationships and how they relate to combat.

distractionary tactics—Various verbal and physical tactics designed to distract your adversary.

double-end bag—A small leather ball hung from the ceiling and anchored to the floor with bungee cord. It helps develop striking accuracy, speed, timing, eye-hand coordination, footwork and overall defensive skills.

double-leg takedown—A takedown that occurs when your opponent shoots for both of your legs to force you to the ground.

E

ectomorph—One of the three somatotypes. A body type characterized by a high degree of slenderness, angularity, and fragility. See endomorph and mesomorph.

effectiveness—One of the three criteria for a CFA body weapon, technique, tactic, or maneuver. It means the ability to produce a desired effect. See efficiency and safety.

efficiency—One of the three criteria for a CFA body weapon, technique, tactic, or maneuver. It means the ability to reach an objective quickly and economically. See effectiveness and safety.

emotionless—A combative attribute. Being temporarily devoid of human feeling.

endomorph—One of the three somatotypes. A body type characterized by a high degree of roundness, softness, and body fat. See ectomorph and mesomorph.

evasion—A defensive maneuver that allows you to strategically maneuver your body away from the assailant's strike.

evasive sidestepping—Evasive footwork where the practitioner moves to either the right or left side.

evasiveness—A combative attribute. The ability to avoid threat or danger.

excessive force—An amount of force that exceeds the need for a particular event and is unjustified in the eyes of the law.

experimentation—The painstaking process of testing a combative hypothesis or theory.

explosiveness—A combative attribute that is characterized by a sudden outburst of violent energy.

F

fear—A strong and unpleasant emotion caused by the anticipation or awareness of threat or danger. There are three stages of fear in order of intensity: fright, panic, and terror. See fright, panic, and terror.

feeder—A skilled technician who manipulates the focus mitts.

femoral nerve—A pressure point area located approximately 6 inches above the knee on the inside of the thigh.

fighting stance—Any one of the stances used in CFA's system. A strategic posture you can assume when face-to-face with an unarmed assailant(s). The fighting stance is generally used after you have launched your first-strike tool.

fight-or-flight syndrome—A response of the sympathetic nervous system to a fearful and threatening situation, during which it prepares your body to either fight or flee from the perceived danger.

finesse—A combative attribute. The ability to skillfully execute a movement or a series of movements with grace and refinement.

first strike—Proactive force used to interrupt the initial stages of an assault before it becomes a self-defense situation.

first-strike principle—A CFA principle that states that when physical danger is imminent and you have no other tactical option but to fight back, you should strike first, strike fast, and strike with authority and keep the pressure on.

first-strike stance—One of the stances used in CFA's system. A strategic posture used prior to initiating a first strike.

first-strike tools—Specific offensive tools designed to initiate a preemptive strike against your adversary.

fisted blows – Hand blows delivered with a clenched fist.

five tactical options – The five strategic responses you can make in a self-defense situation, listed in order of increasing level of resistance: comply, escape, de-escalate, assert, and fight back.

flexibility—The muscles' ability to move through maximum natural ranges. See muscular/skeletal conditioning.

focus mitts—Durable leather hand mitts used to develop and sharpen offensive and defensive skills.

footwork—Quick, economical steps performed on the balls of the feet while you are relaxed, alert, and balanced. Footwork is structured around four general movements: forward, backward, right, and left.

fractal tool—Offensive or defensive tools that can be used in more than one combat range.

fright—The first stage of fear; quick and sudden fear. See panic and terror.

full Beat – One of the four beat classifications in the Widow Maker Program. The full beat strike has a complete initiation and retraction phase.

G

going postal - a slang term referring to a person who suddenly and unexpectedly attacks you with an explosive and frenzied flurry of blows. Also known as postal attack.

grappling range—One of the three ranges of unarmed combat. Grappling range is the closest distance of unarmed combat from which you can employ a wide variety of close-quarter tools and techniques. The grappling range of unarmed combat is also divided into two planes: vertical (standing) and horizontal (ground fighting). See kicking range and punching range.

grappling-range tools—The various body tools and techniques that are employed in the grappling range of unarmed combat, including head butts; biting, tearing, clawing, crushing, and gouging tactics; foot stomps, horizontal, vertical, and diagonal elbow strikes, vertical and diagonal knee strikes, chokes, strangles, joint locks, and holds. See punching range tools and kicking range tools.

ground fighting—Also known as the horizontal grappling plane, this is fighting that takes place on the ground.

guard—Also known as the hand guard, this refers to a fighter's hand positioning.

guard position—Also known as leg guard or scissors hold, this is a ground-fighting position in which a fighter is on his back holding his opponent between his legs.

H

half beat - One of the four beat classifications in the Widow Maker Program. The half beat strike is delivered through the retraction phase of the proceeding strike.

hand positioning—See guard.

hand wraps—Long strips of cotton that are wrapped around the hands and wrists for greater protection.

haymaker—A wild and telegraphed swing of the arms executed by an unskilled fighter.

head-hunter—A fighter who primarily attacks the head.

heavy bag—A large cylindrical bag used to develop kicking, punching, or striking power.

high-line kick—One of the two different classifications of a kick. A kick that is directed to targets above an assailant's waist level. See low-line kick.

hip fusing—A full-contact drill that teaches a fighter to "stand his ground" and overcome the fear of exchanging blows with a stronger opponent. This exercise is performed by connecting two fighters with a 3-foot chain, forcing them to fight in the punching range of unarmed combat.

histrionics—The field of theatrics or acting.

hook kick—A circular kick that can be delivered in both kicking and punching ranges.

hook punch—A circular punch that can be delivered in both the punching and grappling ranges.

I

impact power—Destructive force generated by mass and velocity.

impact training—A training exercise that develops pain tolerance.

incapacitate—To disable an assailant by rendering him unconscious or damaging his bones, joints, or organs.

initiative—Making the first offensive move in combat.

inside position—The area between the opponent's arms, where he has the greatest amount of control.

intent—One of the essential factors to consider when assessing a threatening individual. The assailant's purpose or motive. See demeanor, positioning, range, and weapon capability.

intuition—The innate ability to know or sense something without the use of rational thought.

J

jersey Pull – Strategically pulling the assailant's shirt or jacket over his head as he disengages from the clinch position.

joint lock—A grappling-range technique that immobilizes the assailant's joint.

K

kick—A sudden, forceful strike with the foot.

kicking range—One of the three ranges of unarmed combat. Kicking range is the furthest distance of unarmed combat wherein you use your legs to strike an assailant. See grappling range and punching range.

kicking-range tools—The various body weapons employed in the kicking range of unarmed combat, including side kicks, push kicks, hook kicks, and vertical kicks.

killer instinct—A cold, primal mentality that surges to your consciousness and turns you into a vicious fighter.

kinesics—The study of nonlinguistic body movement communications. (For example, eye movement, shrugs, or facial gestures.)

kinesiology—The study of principles and mechanics of human movement.

kinesthetic perception—The ability to accurately feel your body during the execution of a particular movement.

knowledge—One of the three factors that determine who will win a street fight. Knowledge means knowing and understanding how to fight. See skills and attitude.

L

lead side -The side of the body that faces an assailant.

leg guard—See guard position.

linear movement—Movements that follow the path of a straight line.

low-maintenance tool—Offensive and defensive tools that require the least amount of training and practice to maintain proficiency. Low maintenance tools generally do not require preliminary stretching.

low-line kick—One of the two different classifications of a kick. A kick that is directed to targets below the assailant's waist level. (See high-line kick.)

lock—See joint lock.

M

maneuver—To manipulate into a strategically desired position.

MAP—An acronym that stands for moderate, aggressive, passive. MAP provides the practitioner with three possible responses to various grabs, chokes, and holds that occur from a standing position. See aggressive response, moderate response, and passive response.

Marathon des Sables (MdS) - a six-day, 156-mile ultramarathon held in southern Morocco, in the Sahara Desert. It is considered by many to be the toughest footrace on earth.

martial arts—The "arts of war."

masking—The process of concealing your true feelings from your opponent by manipulating and managing your body language.

mechanics—(See body mechanics.)

mental toughness - a performance mechanism utilizing a collection of mental attributes that allow a person to cope, perform and prevail through the stress of extreme adversity.

mental component—One of the three vital components of the CFA system. The mental component includes the cerebral aspects of fighting including the killer instinct, strategic and tactical development, analysis and integration, philosophy, and cognitive development. See physical component and spiritual component.

mesomorph—One of the three somatotypes. A body type classified by a high degree of muscularity and strength. The mesomorph possesses the ideal physique for unarmed combat. See ectomorph and endomorph.

mobility—A combative attribute. The ability to move your body quickly and freely while balanced. See footwork.

moderate response—One of the three possible counters when assaulted by a grab, choke, or hold from a standing position. Moderate response requires you to counter your opponent with a control and restraint (submission hold). See aggressive response and passive response.

modern martial art—A pragmatic combat art that has evolved to meet the demands and characteristics of the present time.

mounted position—A dominant ground-fighting position where a fighter straddles his opponent.

muscular endurance—The muscles' ability to perform the same

motion or task repeatedly for a prolonged period of time.

muscular flexibility—The muscles' ability to move through maximum natural ranges.

muscular strength—The maximum force that can be exerted by a particular muscle or muscle group against resistance.

muscular/skeletal conditioning—An element of physical fitness that entails muscular strength, endurance, and flexibility.

N

naked choke—A throat choke executed from the chest to back position. This secure choke is executed with two hands and it can be performed while standing, kneeling, and ground fighting with the opponent.

neck crush – A powerful pain compliance technique used when the adversary buries his head in your chest to avoid being razed.

neutralize—See incapacitate.

neutral zone—The distance outside the kicking range at which neither the practitioner nor the assailant can touch the other.

nonaggressive physiology—Strategic body language used prior to initiating a first strike.

nontelegraphic movement—Body mechanics or movements that do not inform an assailant of your intentions.

nuclear ground-fighting tools—Specific grappling range tools designed to inflict immediate and irreversible damage. Nuclear tools and tactics include biting tactics, tearing tactics, crushing tactics, continuous choking tactics, gouging techniques, raking tactics, and all striking techniques.

O

offense—The armed and unarmed means and methods of attacking a criminal assailant.

offensive flow—Continuous offensive movements (kicks, blows, and strikes) with unbroken continuity that ultimately neutralize or terminate the opponent. See compound attack.

offensive reaction time—The elapsed time between target selection and target impaction.

one-mindedness—A state of deep concentration wherein you are free from all distractions (internal and external).

ostrich defense—One of the biggest mistakes one can make when defending against an opponent. This is when the practitioner looks away from that which he fears (punches, kicks, and strikes). His mentality is, "If I can't see it, it can't hurt me."

P

pain tolerance—Your ability to physically and psychologically withstand pain.

panic—The second stage of fear; overpowering fear. See fright and terror.

parry—A defensive technique: a quick, forceful slap that redirects an assailant's linear attack. There are two types of parries: horizontal and vertical.

passive response—One of the three possible counters when assaulted by a grab, choke, or hold from a standing position. Passive response requires you to nullify the assault without injuring your adversary. See aggressive response and moderate response.

patience—A combative attribute. The ability to endure and tolerate difficulty.

perception—Interpretation of vital information acquired from your senses when faced with a potentially threatening situation.

philosophical resolution—The act of analyzing and answering various questions concerning the use of violence in defense of yourself and others.

philosophy—One of the five aspects of CFA's mental component. A deep state of introspection whereby you methodically resolve critical questions concerning the use of force in defense of yourself or others.

physical attributes—The numerous physical qualities that enhance your combative skills and abilities.

physical component—One of the three vital components of the CFA system. The physical component includes the physical aspects of fighting, such as physical fitness, weapon/technique mastery, and combative attributes. See mental component and spiritual component.

physical conditioning—See combative fitness.

physical fitness—See combative fitness.

positional asphyxia—The arrangement, placement, or positioning of your opponent's body in such a way as to interrupt your breathing and cause unconsciousness or possibly death.

positioning—The spatial relationship of the assailant to the assailed person in terms of target exposure, escape, angle of attack, and various other strategic considerations.

postal attack - see going postal.

power—A physical attribute of armed and unarmed combat. The amount of force you can generate when striking an anatomical target.

power generators—Specific points on your body that generate impact power. There are three anatomical power generators: shoulders, hips, and feet.

precision—See accuracy.

preemptive strike—See first strike.

premise—An axiom, concept, rule, or any other valid reason to modify or go beyond that which has been established.

preparedness—A state of being ready for combat. There are three components of preparedness: affective preparedness, cognitive preparedness, and psychomotor preparedness.

probable reaction dynamics - The opponent's anticipated or predicted movements or actions during both armed and unarmed combat.

proficiency training—A CFA training methodology requiring the practitioner to execute a specific body weapon, technique, maneuver, or tactic over and over for a prescribed number of repetitions. See conditioning training and street training.

proxemics—The study of the nature and effect of man's personal space.

proximity—The ability to maintain a strategically safe distance from a threatening individual.

pseudospeciation—A combative attribute. The tendency to assign subhuman and inferior qualities to a threatening assailant.

psychological conditioning—The process of conditioning the mind for the horrors and rigors of real combat.

psychomotor preparedness—One of the three components of preparedness. Psychomotor preparedness means possessing all of the physical skills and attributes necessary to defeat a formidable adversary. See affective preparedness and cognitive preparedness.

punch—A quick, forceful strike of the fists.

punching range—One of the three ranges of unarmed combat. Punching range is the mid range of unarmed combat from which the fighter uses his hands to strike his assailant. See kicking range and grappling range.

punching-range tools—The various body weapons that are employed in the punching range of unarmed combat, including finger jabs, palm-heel strikes, rear cross, knife-hand strikes, horizontal and shovel hooks, uppercuts, and hammer-fist strikes. See grappling-range tools and kicking-range tools.

Q

qualities of combat—See attributes of combat.

quarter beat - One of the four beat classifications of the Widow Maker Program. Quarter beat strikes never break contact with the assailant's face. Quarter beat strikes are primarily responsible for creating the psychological panic and trauma when Razing.

R

range—The spatial relationship between a fighter and a threatening assailant.

range deficiency—The inability to effectively fight and defend in all ranges of combat (armed and unarmed).

range manipulation—A combative attribute. The strategic manipulation of combat ranges.

range proficiency—A combative attribute. The ability to effectively fight and defend in all ranges of combat (armed and unarmed).

ranges of engagement—See combat ranges.

ranges of unarmed combat—The three distances (kicking range, punching range, and grappling range) a fighter might physically engage with an assailant while involved in unarmed combat.

raze – To level, demolish or obliterate.

razer – One who performs the Razing methodology.

razing – The second phase of the Widow Maker Program. A series of vicious close quarter techniques designed to physically and psychologically extirpate a criminal attacker.

razing amplifier - a technique, tactic or procedure that magnifies the destructiveness of your razing technique.

reaction dynamics—see probable reaction dynamics.

reaction time—The elapsed time between a stimulus and the response to that particular stimulus. See offensive reaction time and defensive reaction time.

rear cross—A straight punch delivered from the rear hand that crosses from right to left (if in a left stance) or left to right (if in a right stance).

rear side—The side of the body furthest from the assailant. See lead side.

reasonable force—That degree of force which is not excessive for a particular event and which is appropriate in protecting yourself or others.

refinement—The strategic and methodical process of improving or perfecting.

relocation principle—Also known as relocating, this is a street-fighting tactic that requires you to immediately move to a new location (usually by flanking your adversary) after delivering a compound attack.

repetition—Performing a single movement, exercise, strike, or action continuously for a specific period.

research—A scientific investigation or inquiry.

rhythm—Movements characterized by the natural ebb and flow of related elements.

ritual-oriented training—Formalized training that is conducted without intrinsic purpose. See combat-oriented training and sport-oriented training.

S

safety—One of the three criteria for a CFA body weapon, technique, maneuver, or tactic. It means that the tool, technique, maneuver or tactic provides the least amount of danger and risk for the practitioner. See efficiency and effectiveness.

scissors hold—See guard position.

scorching – Quickly and inconspicuously applying oleoresin capsicum (hot pepper extract) on your fingertips and then razing your adversary.

self-awareness—One of the three categories of CFA awareness. Knowing and understanding yourself. This includes aspects of yourself which may provoke criminal violence and which will promote a proper and strong reaction to an attack. See criminal awareness and situational awareness.

self-confidence—Having trust and faith in yourself.

self-enlightenment—The state of knowing your capabilities, limitations, character traits, feelings, general attributes, and motivations. See self-awareness.

set—A term used to describe a grouping of repetitions.

shadow fighting—A CFA training exercise used to develop and refine your tools, techniques, and attributes of armed and unarmed combat.

sharking – A counter attack technique that is used when your adversary grabs your razing hand.

shielding wedge - a defensive maneuver used to counter an unarmed postal attack.

situational awareness—One of the three categories of CFA awareness. A state of being totally alert to your immediate surroundings, including people, places, objects, and actions. (See criminal awareness and self-awareness.)

skeletal alignment—The proper alignment or arrangement of your body. Skeletal alignment maximizes the structural integrity of striking tools.

skills—One of the three factors that determine who will win a street fight. Skills refers to psychomotor proficiency with the tools and techniques of combat. See Attitude and Knowledge.

slipping—A defensive maneuver that permits you to avoid an assailant's linear blow without stepping out of range. Slipping can be accomplished by quickly snapping the head and upper torso sideways (right or left) to avoid the blow.

snap back—A defensive maneuver that permits you to avoid an assailant's linear and circular blows without stepping out of range. The snap back can be accomplished by quickly snapping the head backward to avoid the assailant's blow.

somatotypes—A method of classifying human body types or builds into three different categories: endomorph, mesomorph, and ectomorph. See endomorph, mesomorph, and ectomorph.

sparring—A training exercise where two or more fighters fight each other while wearing protective equipment.

speed—A physical attribute of armed and unarmed combat. The rate or a measure of the rapid rate of motion.

spiritual component—One of the three vital components of the CFA system. The spiritual component includes the metaphysical issues and aspects of existence. See physical component and mental component.

sport-oriented training—Training that is geared for competition and governed by a set of rules. See combat-oriented training and ritual-oriented training.

sprawling—A grappling technique used to counter a double- or single-leg takedown.

square off—To be face-to-face with a hostile or threatening assailant who is about to attack you.

stance—One of the many strategic postures you assume prior to or during armed or unarmed combat.

stick fighting—Fighting that takes place with either one or two sticks.

strategic positioning—Tactically positioning yourself to either escape, move behind a barrier, or use a makeshift weapon.

strategic/tactical development—One of the five elements of CFA's mental component.

strategy—A carefully planned method of achieving your goal of engaging an assailant under advantageous conditions.

street fight—A spontaneous and violent confrontation between two or more individuals wherein no rules apply.

street fighter—An unorthodox combatant who has no formal training. His combative skills and tactics are usually developed in the street by the process of trial and error.

street training—A CFA training methodology requiring the practitioner to deliver explosive compound attacks for 10 to 20 seconds. See condition ng training and proficiency training.

Printed in Great Britain
by Amazon

68064034R00142

strength training—The process of developing muscular strength through systematic application of progressive resistance.

stress - physiological and psychological arousal caused by a stressor.

stressors - any activity, situation, circumstance, event, experience, or condition that causes a person to experience both physiological and psychological stress.

striking art—A combat art that relies predominantly on striking techniques to neutralize or terminate a criminal attacker.

striking shield—A rectangular shield constructed of foam and vinyl used to develop power in your kicks, punches, and strikes.

striking tool—A natural body weapon that impacts with the assailant's anatomical target.

strong side—The strongest and most coordinated side of your body.

structure—A definite and organized pattern.

style—The distinct manner in which a fighter executes or performs his combat skills.

stylistic integration—The purposeful and scientific collection of tools and techniques from various disciplines, which are strategically integrated and dramatically altered to meet three essential criteria: efficiency, effectiveness, and combative safety.

submission holds—Also known as control and restraint techniques, many of these locks and holds create sufficient pain to cause the adversary to submit.

system—The unification of principles, philosophies, rules, strategies, methodologies, tools, and techniques of a particular method of combat.

T

tactic—The skill of using the available means to achieve an end.

target awareness—A combative attribute that encompasses five strategic principles: target orientation, target recognition, target selection, target impaction, and target exploitation.

target exploitation—A combative attribute. The strategic maximization of your assailant's reaction dynamics during a fight. Target exploitation can be applied in both armed and unarmed encounters.

target impaction—The successful striking of the appropriate anatomical target.

target orientation—A combative attribute. Having a workable knowledge of the assailant's anatomical targets.

target recognition—The ability to immediately recognize appropriate anatomical targets during an emergency self-defense situation.

target selection—The process of mentally selecting the appropriate anatomical target for your self-defense situation. This is predicated on certain factors, including proper force response, assailant's positioning, and range.

target stare—A form of telegraphing in which you stare at the anatomical target you intend to strike.

target zones—The three areas in which an assailant's anatomical targets are located. (See zone one, zone two and zone three.)

technique—A systematic procedure by which a task is accomplished.

telegraphic cognizance—A combative attribute. The ability to recognize both verbal and non-verbal signs of aggression or assault.

telegraphing—Unintentionally making your intentions known to your adversary.

tempo—The speed or rate at which you speak.

terminate—To kill.

terror—The third stage of fear; defined as overpowering fear. See fright and panic.

timing—A physical and mental attribute of armed and unarmed combat. Your ability to execute a movement at the optimum moment.

tone—The overall quality or character of your voice.

tool—See body weapon.

traditional martial arts—Any martial art that fails to evolve and change to meet the demands and characteristics of its present environment.

traditional style/system—See traditional martial arts.

training drills—The various exercises and drills aimed at perfecting combat skills, attributes, and tactics.

trap and tuck – A counter move technique used when the adversary attempts to raze you during your quarter beat assault.

U

unified mind—A mind free and clear of distractions and focused on the combative situation.

use of force response—A combative attribute. Selecting the appropriate level of force for a particular emergency self-defense situation.

V

viciousness—A combative attribute. The propensity to be extremely violent and destructive often characterized by intense savagery.

violence—The intentional utilization of physical force to coerce, injure, cripple, or kill.

visualization—Also known as mental visualization or mental imagery. The purposeful formation of mental images and scenarios in the mind's eye.

W

warm-up—A series of mild exercises, stretches, and movements designed to prepare you for more intense exercise.

weak side—The weaker and more uncoordinated side of your body.

weapon and technique mastery—A component of CFA's physical component. The kinesthetic and psychomotor development of a weapon or combative technique.

weapon capability—An assailant's ability to use and attack with a particular weapon.

webbing - The first phase of the Widow Maker Program. Webbing is a two hand strike delivered to the assailant's chin. It is called Webbing because your hands resemble a large web that wraps around the enemy's face.

widow maker – One who makes widows by destroying husbands.

widow maker program – A CFA combat program specifically designed to teach the law abiding citizen how to use extreme force when faced with immediate threat of unlawful deadly criminal attack. The Widow Maker program is divided into two phases or methodologies: Webbing and Razing.

Y

yell—A loud and aggressive scream or shout used for various strategic reasons.

Z

zero beat – One of the four beat classifications of the Widow Maker, Feral Fighting and Savage Street Fighting Programs. Zero beat strikes are full pressure techniques applied to a specific target until it completely ruptures. They include gouging, crushing, biting, and choking techniques.

zone one—Anatomical targets related to your senses, including the eyes, temple, nose, chin, and back of neck.

zone three—Anatomical targets related to your mobility, including thighs, knees, shins, and instep.

zone two—Anatomical targets related to your breathing, including front of neck, solar plexus, ribs, and groin.

Photo Credits

- *Page 10: Photo by AJ Guel.*

- *Page 14: Photo by Staff Sgt. Michael L. Casteel, U.S. Army*

- *Page 15: Photo by Staff Sgt. Shawn Weismiller*

- *Page 16: Photo by Mass Communication Specialist 1st Class Sean Mulligan*

- *Page 17: Photo by Sgt. Scott Schmidt*

- *Page 22: Photo by John Loo*

- *Page 30: Courtesy wikipedia by Crs9740*

- *Page 31: Photo by Chad Cooper*

- *Page 32: Photo by Scott Calleja*

- *Page 79: Photo by Mass Communication Specialist 2nd Class Shauntae Hinkle-Lymas*

- *Page 80: Photo by Spc. Joshua Leonard*

- *Page 81: Courtesy Wikimedia Commons, photo by Gensanders*

- *Page 83: Courtesy US Army*

- *Page 87: Photo by Sgt. Susan Wilt*

- *Page 88: Courtesy Unites States Department of Defense*

- *Page 89: Photo by Lance Cpl. Ismael Ortega*

About Sammy Franco

With over 30 years of experience, Sammy Franco is one of the world's foremost authorities on armed and unarmed self-defense. Highly regarded as a leading innovator in combat sciences, Mr. Franco was one of the premier pioneers in the field of "reality-based" self-defense and combat instruction.

Sammy Franco is perhaps best known as the founder and creator of Contemporary Fighting Arts (CFA), a state-of-the-art offensive-based combat system that is specifically designed for real-world self-defense. CFA is a sophisticated and practical system of self-defense, designed specifically to provide efficient and effective methods to avoid, defuse, confront, and neutralize both armed and unarmed attackers.

Sammy Franco has frequently been featured in martial art magazines, newspapers, and appeared on numerous radio and television programs. Mr. Franco has also authored numerous books, magazine articles, and editorials and has developed a popular library of instructional videos.

Sammy Franco's experience and credibility in the combat science is unequaled. One of his many accomplishments in this field includes the fact that he has earned the ranking of a Law Enforcement Master Instructor, and has designed, implemented, and taught officer survival training to the United States Border Patrol (USBP). He has instructed members of the US Secret Service, Military Special Forces,

237

Washington DC Police Department, Montgomery County, Maryland Deputy Sheriffs, and the US Library of Congress Police. Sammy Franco is also a member of the prestigious International Law Enforcement Educators and Trainers Association (ILEETA) as well as the American Society of Law Enforcement Trainers (ASLET) and he is listed in the "Who's Who Director of Law Enforcement Instructors."

Sammy Franco is also a nationally certified Law Enforcement Instructor in the following curricula: PR-24 Side-Handle Baton, Police Arrest and Control Procedures, Police Personal Weapons Tactics, Police Power Handcuffing Methods, Police Oleoresin Capsicum Aerosol Training (OCAT), Police Weapon Retention and Disarming Methods, Police Edged Weapon Countermeasures and "Use of Force" Assessment and Response Methods.

Mr. Franco regularly conducts dynamic and enlightening seminars on different aspects of combat training, mental toughness and achieving personal peak performance.

On a personal level, Sammy Franco is an animal lover, who will go to great lengths to assist and rescue animals. Throughout the years, he's rescued everything from turkey vultures to goats. However, his most treasured moments are always spent with his beloved German Shepherd dogs.

For more information about Mr. Franco, you can visit his website at **SammyFranco.com** or follow him on Twitter **@RealSammyFranco**

Other Books by Sammy Franco

THE WIDOW MAKER PROGRAM
Extreme Self-Defense for Deadly Force Situations
by Sammy Franco

The Widow Maker Program is a shocking and revolution-ary fighting style designed to unleash extreme force when faced with the immediate threat of an unlawful deadly criminal attack. In this unique book, self-defense innova-tor Sammy Franco teaches you his brutal and unorthodox combat style that is virtually indefensible and utterly dev-astating. With over 250 photographs and detailed step-by-step instructions, The Widow Maker Program teaches you Franco's surreptitious Webbing and Razing techniques. When combined, these two fighting methods create an unstoppable force capable of destroying the toughest adversary. 8.5 x 5.5, paperback, photos, illus, 218 pages.

FERAL FIGHTING
Advanced Widow Maker Fighting Techniques
by Sammy Franco

In this sequel, Sammy Franco marches forward with cutting-edge concepts and techniques that will take your self-defense skills to entirely new levels of combat performance. Feral Fighting includes Franco's revolutionary Shielding Wedge technique. When used correctly, it transforms you into an unstoppable human meat grinder, capable of destroying any criminal adversary. Feral Fighting also teaches you the cunning art or Scorching. Learn how to convert your fingertips into burning torches that generate over 2 million scoville heat units causing excruciating pain and temporarily blindness. 8.5 x 5.5, paperback, photos, illustrations, 204 pages.

MAXIMUM DAMAGE
Hidden Secrets Behind Brutal
Fighting Combination
by Sammy Franco

Maximum Damage teaches you the quickest ways to beat your opponent in the street by exploiting his physical and psychological reactions in a fight. Learn how to stay two steps ahead of your adversary by knowing exactly how he will react to your strikes before they are delivered. In this unique book, reality based self-defense expert Sammy Franco reveals his unique Probable Reaction Dynamic (PRD) fighting method. Probable reaction dynamics are both a scientific and comprehensive offensive strategy based on the positional theory of combat. Regardless of your style of fighting, PRD training will help you overpower your opponent by seamlessly integrating your strikes into brutal fighting combinations that are fast, ferocious and final! 8.5 x 5.5, paperback, 240 photos, illustrations, 238 pages.

SAVAGE STREET FIGHTING
Tactical Savagery as a Last Resort
by Sammy Franco

In this revolutionary book, Sammy Franco reveals the science behind his most primal street fighting method. Savage Street Fighting is a brutal self-defense system specifically designed to teach the law-abiding citizen how to use "Tactical Savagery" when faced with the immediate threat of an unlawful deadly criminal attack. Savage Street Fighting is systematically engineered to protect you when there are no other self-defense options left! With over 300 photographs and detailed step-by-step instructions, Savage Street Fighting is a must-have book for anyone concerned about real world self-defense. Now is the time to learn how to unleash your inner beast! 8.5 x 5.5, paperback, 317 photos, illustrations, 232 pages.

FIRST STRIKE
End a Fight in Ten Seconds or Less!
by Sammy Franco

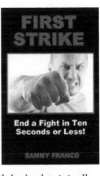

Learn how to stop any attack before it starts by mastering the art of the preemptive strike. First Strike gives you an easy-to-learn yet highly effective self-defense game plan for handling violent close-quarter combat encounters. First Strike will teach you instinctive, practical and realistic self-defense techniques that will drop any criminal attacker to the floor with one punishing blow. By reading this book and by practicing, you will learn the hard-hitting skills necessary to execute a punishing first strike and ultimately prevail in a self-defense situation. And that's what it is all about: winning in as little time as possible. 8.5 x 5.5, paperback, photos, illustrations, 202 pages.

WAR MACHINE
How to Transform Yourself Into A Vicious & Deadly Street Fighter
by Sammy Franco

War Machine is a book that will change you for the rest of your life! When followed accordingly, War Machine will forge your mind, body and spirit into iron. Once armed with the mental and physical attributes of the War Machine, you will become a strong and confident warrior that can handle just about anything that life may throw your way. In essence, War

Machine is a way of life. Powerful, intense, and hard. 11 x 8.5, paperback, photos, illustrations, 210 pages.

KUBOTAN POWER
Quick and Simple Steps to Mastering the Kubotan Keychain
by Sammy Franco

With over 290 photographs and step-by-step instructions, Kubotan Power is the authoritative resource for mastering this devastating self-defense weapon. In this one-of-a-kind book, world-renowned self-defense expert, Sammy Franco takes thirty years of real-world teaching experience and gives you quick, easy and practical kubotan techniques that can be used by civilians, law enforcement personnel, or military professionals. The Kubotan is an incredible self-defense weapon that has helped thousands of people effectively defend themselves. Men, women, law enforcement officers, military, and security professionals alike, appreciate this small and discreet self-defense tool. Unfortunately, however, very little has been written about the kubotan, leaving it shrouded in both mystery and ignorance. As a result, most people don't know how to unleash the full power of this unique personal defense weapon. 8.5 x 5.5, paperback, 290 photos, illustrations, 204 pages.

THE COMPLETE BODY OPPONENT BAG BOOK
by Sammy Franco

In this one-of-a-kind book, Sammy Franco teaches you the many hidden training features of the body opponent bag that will improve your fighting skills and boost your conditioning. With detailed photographs, step-by-step instructions, and dozens of unique workout routines, The Complete Body Opponent Bag Book is the authoritative resource for mastering this lifelike punching bag. The Complete Body Opponent Bag Book covers stances, punching, kicking, grappling techniques, mobility and footwork, targets, fighting ranges, training gear, time based workouts, punching and kicking combinations, weapons training, grappling drills, ground fighting, and dozens of workouts that will challenge you for years to come. 8.5 x 5.5, paperback, 139 photos, illustrations, 206 pages.

CONTEMPORARY FIGHTING ARTS, LLC
"Real World Self-Defense Since 1989"
www.SammyFranco.com